From Principles to Best Practices
A "Making Markets Matter" Guide
to Managing African Agribusinesses

Edited by:
Ralph D. Christy
Mohammad Karaan
Edward Mabaya
Krisztina Z. Tihanyi

Market Matters Inc.
401 S. Albany Street
Ithaca, NY 14850 USA
http://marketmattersinc.org

First printing 2015.
Market Matters Inc.

ISBN: 0692417346
ISBN-13: 978-0692417348 (Market Matters Inc.)

DEDICATION

To African entrepreneurs:
"Creators of economic opportunity"

CONTENTS

ACKNOWLEDGEMENTS

This edited volume is the result of the efforts of many individuals and organizations who share a common view that small and medium enterprises in Africa deserve more attention and support than they currently receive. We owe a huge debt to those individuals and organizations, one that we can only repay by continuing the work of strengthening the capacity of African agribusinesses and improving the environment within which they operate.

In September 2001 the first Making Markets Matter program was launched on the campus of Stellenbosch University. During that fateful week, little did we know that we were embarking on a 15-year journey that would foster enduring relationships among a talented group of scholars and business thought-leaders, build a network among African businesses across countries, and challenge the conventional wisdom of business management principles offered to managers in industrial nations. Over the years we have gained much from our engagement with participating agribusinesses through discussions, case study development, and technical assistance; therefore, our largest degree of gratitude is reserved for the thousands of businesses who have shared with us their realities of operating an agribusiness in Africa. You have generously shared with us your success stories, disappointments, heartbreaks, and insights on operating businesses in Africa. All of the authors of this volume feel fortunate to have been a part of this experience.

We also are immensely grateful to MMM facilitators, who all share a deep love for Africa and Africa's development and who generously volunteer their amazing talents and time for our program each year. Beyond the facilitators who authored chapters in this volume, we would like to thank Natasha Blackshear, Michael Brown, Joyce Cacho, Joyce Chitja, Ernie Davis, Carlos da Silva, Dilip Gokhale, Liezl Hobson, Steven Hobson, Angela Ichwan, Andrew Jackson, Willene Johnson, Leapetswe Malete, Margaret Matanda, Brian Meyer, Nomathemba Mhlanga, Emelly Mutambatsere, Lulama Ndibongo Traub, Pete Ondeng, Frank Pedraza, Sally Pedraza, Robert Rugimbana, Kenneth Robinson, Eugene Terry, Norma Tregurtha, Johan van Rooyen, Nick Vink, Dave Weatherspoon, and Mark Wenner, who all contributed in ways that enriched Making Markets Matter and offered an important source of advice for MMM participants beyond the program. Over the years, we became valued colleagues and friends, providing support when needed and celebrating each other's personal and professional accomplishments. Thank you.

On the first day of each Making Markets Matter program, we give participants a challenge -- to secure three business deals by the end of the week! Entrepreneurs take this challenge seriously, and their efforts have resulted in innumerable business transactions and joint-ventures that we are very proud of witnessing but cannot fully take credit for. As we ask participants at the end of the week to report whether they were able to close on the three business deals, we are always taken aback by the level of enthusiasm they exude about potential deals they have made during the program. Even more surprising, we have also witnessed the formation of joint-ventures between MMM companies. Wow, our companies are having companies! Thank you.

We believe that the courageous women and men who seek to achieve their business goals in an environment of uncertainty, perhaps one that is more uncertain than any other business environment on the planet, have something special to offer to the study of business management. Challenges such as fragile infrastructure, uncertain political environments, questionable access to technology, and an ever-changing natural environment that includes climate change – all forces beyond the entrepreneurs' control - present unbelievable uncertainty and a lack of control to producers, valued-added manufacturers, and service providers along the food and fiber value-chain in Africa. Their ability to not only survive but thrive under uncertain conditions, in our collective assessment, elevates their shared stories into important lessons for business managers globally. Modern business management, as taught in industrial nations, assumes a degree of "control" and "certainty"—

neither of which are common in operating an enterprises in Africa. As we have learned from MMM participants, because of the unique business environment, conventional business principles may or may not work in the African context. We are fortunate to have learned important lessons from the owners of African enterprises, and our effort to capture their insights and lessons herein is our small way of showing our appreciation to the MMM participants. Thank you.

We too are fortunate to be affiliated with institutions like Cornell and Stellenbosch Universities. Both universities provided support early on and nurtured our dreams and ideas that have become a successful executive agribusiness education program in Africa and now an edited volume that captures important marketing management lessons from the continent.

Our journey has just begun, and we look forward to many more years of Making Markets Matter with African agribusiness SMEs!

PREFACE

The Story behind a Name: What is Making Markets Matter?

In 2001 two leading academic institutions, Cornell University (USA) and Stellenbosch University (South Africa), recognized the need for high-quality and comprehensive agribusiness training programs serving small and medium enterprises (SMEs) in emerging markets. This recognition led to the birth of Making Markets Matter (MMM)—an agribusiness training program that provides an introduction to the building blocks of business management, along with opportunities to network with industry stakeholders, fellow business leaders, and other agribusiness practitioners. Within two years of the inaugural program, MMM outgrew its academic home, and Market Matters Inc., a nonprofit organization, was formed to coordinate the program series and other related activities. To date, MMM programs have been offered in Africa; the flagship program takes place in South Africa every year, while a number of satellite programs have been held in other African countries and for specific groups or industries (e.g., women entrepreneurs, value-added food manufacturers, seed companies, etc.). In its 15-year span the program has engaged over 2,000 businesses; what started as a small initiative with 30 participants has grown into a well-known and respected agribusiness training program in Africa. (See Figure 1 for the countries and sectors represented in MMM to date.)

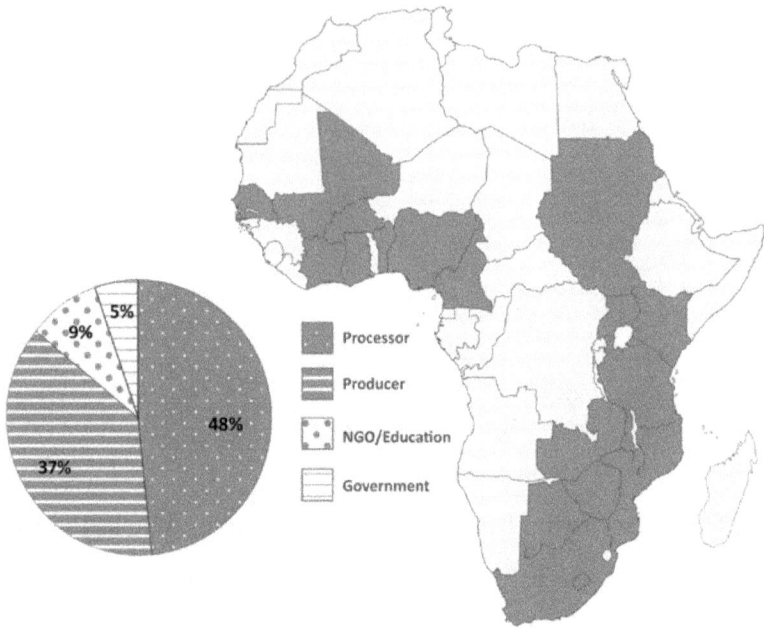

Figure 1: MMM participants by geographic and sector representation.

A unique aspect of each Making Markets Matter program is its facilitators, an international group of experts who are all recognized thought leaders in their respective fields and who all share a commitment and passion for African development. This passion explains why many of them return year after year to volunteer their time and talents in the program. During the course of the program, participants are encouraged to approach facilitators with specific questions about their businesses, taking advantage of such one-on-on consultations. Judging by the feedback from participants, this opportunity to interact with facilitators is one of the program's highlights for the entrepreneurs. Facilitators, too, value getting to know participants and learning about their businesses. Thus, each MMM program fosters an exchange of ideas and experiences. In fact, this give-and-take between facilitator and participant has at times required the facilitator to become the "student"—listening to acquire a greater understanding of participants' insights that challenge conventional business wisdom.

Through those exchanges important lessons have emerged and crystallized about the political, economic, social, and cultural realities of

African countries that influence the ways SMEs can—and do—conduct business that are, in many cases, local adaptations of so-called standard business practices. These lessons include the observation that many SMEs compete with one another on non-price attributes of their products. They achieve their organizational goals by experimenting, by product development strategies, and by positioning their products in the marketplace. Second, while many firms aspire to sell their products in international markets, others, increasingly, subscribe to the view that "all markets matter" and therefore opt to position their enterprise to take advantage of growing opportunities in local urban or regional markets. When companies do export, they usually do so through a strong relationship with a single buyer located in a distant market, often in developed countries. Over the years it has also become clear that SMEs in emerging markets use unique strategies because they are forced to accept a greater degree of uncertainty than their counterparts in developed countries. Finally, we have learned that within African small-scale enterprises, leadership is an integral part of strategy, as many companies were created by visionary men and women who are also leaders in their respective communities.

In response to these lessons MMM facilitators have tailored the standard modules to make them applicable and meaningful in a developing-country/emerging-market context. In addition, it became clear that, for the MMM program to be truly transformative, it needed to explore with participating SMEs a deeper, more reflective understanding of the realities of operating a business in Africa. The program answered this challenge by expanding its offering to "soft skills" such as gender dynamics, family business, business negotiations, and business ethics.

In addition to "classroom" sessions, each MMM program is also a venue for network building: participating companies have many opportunities to interact with one another and to explore the potential for new business partnerships. Besides networking with fellow companies, participants also have the opportunity to meet representatives of the wider agribusiness industry: each year the program also includes invited speakers from food retailers, financial entities, or development institutions who often talk about ways in which agribusiness SMEs can access markets, financing, and other useful tools. We take the networking aspect of the program just as seriously as its formal class discussions. Each year we challenge participants to leave the program with three business deals secured.

The 15th anniversary of our program has prompted us to reflect on valuable lessons learned to date, and we decided to share those lessons with a wider audience in the form of this book. The book project began by inviting MMM facilitators to contribute a chapter on a topic related to their expertise. Each chapter has three interrelated objectives: one is to introduce the reader to useful principles, concepts, frameworks, and tools related to a particular functional area of the business (e.g., planning, marketing, cash flow, human management, etc.). The second aim is to home in on key differences that shape the environment or context for African agribusiness SMEs setting them apart from other parts of the world. And third, chapters endeavor to present "best practices" African SMEs may use to overcome the unique environmental challenges of doing business in Africa.

Objectives

The overarching goal of this book is to share best practices of building and running small and medium agribusinesses in Africa with a wide range of readers, especially those who currently own or manage their business and those who are strongly thinking about owning their own business. The specific objectives are to:

- Understand and capture the realities of how local political, economic, social, and cultural factors influence the ways in which agribusiness SMEs are run in Africa. Focusing on a host of topics ranging from marketing to business strategy, from human resource management to family business, the book provides rich detail, gleaned from extensive interactions with SMEs on the ground.
- Adapt "standard" business market management principles to fit the realities of SME owners and managers in Africa.
- Offer information that is applicable and accessible to a variety of audiences, ranging from business owners and managers to academics in charge of agribusiness training programs—and all interested parties in-between.
- Spark further conversation about managing African businesses by inviting others to contribute their experiences through crowdsourcing once the book has been published.

Our Target Audience

This book shares the wealth of experience amassed by MMM facilitators over 15 years, and its goal is to share this collective knowledge in a form that is easily accessible to all interested readers and that is practical and timely. Importantly, through the use of online communication technologies, we hope to make the book a starting point of further conversations about starting and running SMEs in Africa. This should be especially useful as the African business environment is dynamic and its understanding requires frequent assessments.

We envision the primary audience for this book to be SME owners and managers in Africa who are looking for business management advice with a special lens focusing on the African context. But understanding these local realities is important for anyone in charge of a Business Development Services training program or those wishing to do business with SMEs in Africa. Learning about the local realities may be valuable as it may validate readers' experiences in ways that build confidence—or, as the case may be, accounts of different best practices may provide food for thought and alternatives to existing practices.

A Quick Word about Definitions

Although all of the authors have an academic background, strictly speaking this book is purposefully nonacademic. Rather its aim is precisely to capture principles, concepts, and tools in ways that are useful in an SME setting. For this reason, the emphasis is on conveying the main concepts, as opposed to delving into the finer details of those concepts. Terminology, while not chosen without careful thought, is also used a bit more loosely. Some of the key terms are listed below.

- Small and medium enterprise: The fundamental criterion to determine whether a business qualifies as an SME is size, i.e., the number of employees. The threshold numbers cited vary by region, however, that is, a small company in Europe or North America may be considered medium size by African standards. For this reason, perhaps the most helpful definition for us is to refer to the companies we have worked with in Making Markets Matter, most of which have between 3 and 10 full-time employees, the largest ones employing up to 25 permanent staff.

- Agribusiness refers to agriculture-related enterprises that span the range from primary production to value-added products along the food and fiber value chains.
- Business/company/ enterprise: Although in certain contexts these terms have specific definitions that denote size and complexity, here they are used somewhat interchangeably in order to make the text readable and less repetitious. The context reveals what type of enterprise we are talking about, and in the majority of cases it is a small or medium-sized agro-enterprise. Similarly, the words agro-enterprise, agribusiness, and agripreneurship (and their derivatives) are used to refer to similar entities, again to avoid repetition in the text.

The topics covered in this book are by no means exhaustive, but rather evolved from the interactions between our facilitators and workshop participants. As such, this book covers four core areas of business management: strategic thinking, marketing strategy, financial management, and human resource management. In addition to those core areas, we have selected three topics of interest to SMEs—indigenous food product development, the dynamics of running a family business, and the impact of gender on agribusiness SMEs in Africa. It is our hope that this book will be a starting point of many more conversations about managing agribusiness SMEs in Africa.

Ralph D. Christy
Mohammad Karaan
Edward Mabaya
Krisztina Tihanyi

Ithaca, NY, USA
April 2015

MARKET-ORIENTATED STRATEGIC THINKING

Ralph D. Christy, Mohammad Karaan, and Norbert Wilson

Introduction

Strategic thinking, a widely used business management process, has evolved globally over time into a set of tools enterprises use to plan their future. For many enterprises, the need to formally consider their future arises from a period of slowed or stalled growth—a moment of near-panic that requires fresh thinking about new pathways to improve the company's performance. The goal of the strategic thinking process is to develop and implement procedures that will shape and reshape the company so that it will experience satisfactory profits and growth. Effective strategic thinking will help develop and maintain a viable fit between the objectives and resources of the company. Strategic thinking is useful for managers of all business sizes, operating in different industries and countries of varying levels of economic development.

Enterprises that follow effective strategies stake a clear market position and in turn their goals and business practices are visible to their stakeholders. A clear and visible strategic plan signals to your customers that you have "your act together," and actions resulting from clear strategic plans are reassuring to your customers as well as your employees. It will help you compete successfully and help you achieve your organizational goals. In short, a company's strategic plan for growth and profitability is its "game plan" (Kotler 2012).

While having such a game plan has many positive results—creating a market position, pleasing customers, motivating employees, and achieving organizational goals—in our experience, few African enterprises purposefully engage in strategic thinking. Each year company owners and managers in our Making Markets Matter training program report that they simply do not have sufficient time to "think about the future" when they are surrounded by "sharks"—daily challenges that seem to require immediate responses. They feel that the day-to-day running of their business fully engages all of their resources, diverting time and energy from formulating formal strategies that can grow their company (Mankins and Steele 2006). Yet others report that they are unfamiliar with strategic thinking processes and lack the managerial skills to engage in such activities.

But there is another important reason that gets in the way of strategic thinking, one that often goes unsaid until one probes deeper—a lack of trust and openness between owners/managers and employees. Trust and openness are two key elements of the strategic thinking process, which involves an open and honest conversation with important stakeholders about the future direction of the company. Many African owners/managers find this difficult to do, and when asked why, the most common response is that discussing the future direction of their company is above the "pay grade" of their employees; owners/managers do not think their employees should have formal input into the strategic decisions about the enterprise's future.

In contrast, most managers are more willing to discuss with their employees the enterprise's marketing strategy. While the strategic thinking process involves broad values that chart the future direction of the company, marketing strategy, which gives priority to the daily implementation of marketing strategies—those concerning the pricing, placement, promotion, and appearance of the product—seems easier to broach with employees. In short, it seems easier for owners and senior managers to engage in a discussion about the more immediate, tactical side of running the company than it is to engage in discussions about its long-term direction.

Is market-oriented strategic thinking an appropriate management process in Africa? If so, how can we make strategic thinking more useful to owners of African enterprises? To respond to those questions, this chapter first presents the essential elements of strategic thinking all enterprises should be familiar with. Next, based on our interactions with the 2000 or so enterprises that have participated in our programs, we present 10 best practices (and principles) that we think can make the strategic thinking process more relevant and applicable to African small and medium enterprises (SMEs).

Strategic Thinking: Concept, Conceptual Framework, and Context

Strategic thinking involves the fundamental rethinking, and sometimes radical redesign, of business processes to achieve dramatic improvement in critical measures of performance (cost, quality, service, speed, growth, and profit). How do enterprises formally develop and implement strategic thinking processes in their organizations? On a fundamental level, strategic thinking requires a company to consider three burning questions: Who are we? Where are we going? And, how will we get there? On the following pages, we will turn to these questions one at a time.

Who Are We?

In answering the question "Who are we?" enterprises must identify the elements that give them identity. In the formal economy, organizations—including enterprises—have legal documents such as articles of incorporation and by-laws to establish their legal identity. These documents set the foundation for the company's legal identity and how it is managed (e.g., how directors are elected, how meetings of directors and shareholders are conducted, what officers the organization will have and a description of their duties).

A key piece of the answer to this question lies in the enterprise's mission statement—a written summary of its broad purpose and the general criteria for assessing its long-term effectiveness. Mission statements should answer the following general questions:

- What is your business?
- Who is your customer?
- What is of value to the customer?
- What will your business be?
- What should your business be?

A mission statement should be motivating and should stress major policies your company wants to honor. It should provide a vision and direction for the strategic goals of your company (Kotler 2012).

Although having a well-developed mission statement is important, to think strategically you must operate within the current context of your company's situation while keeping an eye on the future; otherwise you are simply a dreamer. What are your company's realities? What trends might influence its future? To answer these questions, your company has several frameworks to choose from. Perhaps the most commonly used are the SWOT and PEST analyses.

SWOT Analysis

The SWOT analysis considers the internal (strengths and weaknesses) and external (opportunities and threats) factors that help or hinder your company's ability to achieve its goals (Figure 1). The internal factors are within the company's control (that is, those are things you and your employees can do something about), while the external factors are often beyond your control, yet very important for you to be aware of.

	Helpful	Harmful
Within company control	Strengths	Weaknesses
Beyond company control	Opportunities	Threats

Figure 1. SWOT analysis

As you conduct a SWOT analysis, you may find it useful to consider the following questions—and add your own, as needed.

Questions about internal factors:
- What is our product/service and who are the customers we hope to reach?
- How do we know if our product/service satisfies the desires of our customers?
- How does our product/service reach our customers?
- Why do we use this method to reach our customers?

Questions about external factors:
- What are the characteristics of our competitors?
- How is our product/service different from the product/service of our competitors?
- Which government policies affect our product/service?

Questions about both internal and external factors:

- How will our previous responses change in the next year? In the next five years?

Table 1 presents an example of a SWOT analysis, listing general terms that a company may identify. Your SWOT analysis, of course, may—and probably should—be more specific (e.g., when you say "changing customer tastes," be sure you know how those tastes are changing exactly).

Table 1. SWOT analysis factors

Strengths	Weaknesses
• Strong brand name • Good customer reputation • Exclusive access to resources or distribution networks • Managerial expertise • Patents or copyrights	• Limited operational capacity • Poor customer reputation • Limited cash flow or other financial resources • Lack of management capabilities
Opportunities	**Threats**
• Unfulfilled customer needs • New technology development • Industry or lifestyle trends • Loosening government regulation • Trade barrier removal	• Changing customer tastes • New government regulation • Increased trade barriers • Emerging substitute products • Competition/Competitors?

Although the SWOT analysis is used widely for the evaluation of a company's position, it does not provide a complete appraisal. Strategy is an attempt to hit a moving target, and SWOT is not very effective at factoring in the uncertainty often associated with this movement. Here is where another tool, the PEST analysis, may be useful.

PEST Analysis

An often used complement to the SWOT, the PEST analysis framework helps managers gain insight into the forces and trends influencing their company's future. An acronym for four sets of forces (**p**olitical, **e**conomic, **s**ocial, and **t**echnological; sometimes also referred to as STEP), this framework enables managers to identify and assess external forces that are beyond the company's control, but which nevertheless may affect the company's ability to obtain its goals. Table 2 provides an example of a PEST analysis. Of course, with each of these factors, it is important to know precisely how these factors affects the business.

Table 2. PEST analysis

Political Factors	Economic Factors
• Trade laws and regulations • Political stability • Wage and labor regulations	• Taxation • Market intervention • Economic growth • Interest and inflation rates
Social Factors	**Technological Factors**
• Education • Culture • Demographics • Gender	• Research and development • Technology transfer rate • Energy costs and availability • Information and communication technologies

Where Are We Going?

Once an analysis of the present situation of your enterprise is complete, you must establish strategies for future action. Using the information generated through a situation analysis, your next task is to establish your enterprise's goals and corresponding objectives to move forward strategically. Table 3 provides a list of common corporate goals, categorized by type.

It is important to distinguish between goals and objectives. Goals are the end results you want to achieve; they provide focus and purpose. In turn, objectives are specific steps you must take to reach your goals. One way to distinguish goals from objectives is to ask: Is this an end or a means to an end? Goals are an end; objectives are means to those ends, the steps you need to take to reach your goal. To be most useful, your company's goals must be "SMART"—specific, measurable, achievable, realistic, and timely.

Growth vs. Consolidation

Organizations typically choose one of two directions when selecting a corporate strategy: growth or consolidation. As you will see in a moment, growth strategies can take many different forms, but the overall aim is to grow the company through either new products, new markets, or both.

Table 3. Common types of corporate goals

Profitability
- Net profit as a percentage of sales
- Net profit as a percentage of total investment
- Net profit per share of common stock

Volume
- Market share
- Percentage growth in sales
- Sales rank in market
- Production capacity utilization

Stability
- Variance in annual sales volume
- Variance in seasonal sales volume
- Variance in profitability

Non-financial
- Maintenance of family control
- Improved corporate image
- Enhancement of technology or quality of life

Source: Guiltinan and Paul (1991)

Consolidation strategies, in contrast, essentially scale back the company by reducing the number of products, employees, its market share, or a combination of these. Let us start with growth strategies.

Growth strategies can be implemented for current or new markets. Growth strategies for current markets include market penetration, product development, and vertical integration. Growth strategies for new markets comprise market development, market expansion, diversification, and strategic alliances.

One of the most commonly used tools for identifying a growth strategy for your company is the Ansoff framework (Figure 2). Igor Ansoff, considered the father of strategic management, first published the product-market matrix in 1957 in the *Harvard Business Review*. Though this strategic matrix was published over 50 years ago, it is still widely used today to identify a growth strategy via the firm's current and potential products and markets. The Ansoff framework considers four possible corporate strategies:

- *Market penetration:* A strategy by which a firm makes an effort to increase sales of existing products in its current markets. Usually accomplished through increased promotion or lowering prices.
- *Product development:* A strategy by which a firm develops new products for its existing market(s). Usually implemented because of changing technologies or customer tastes.
- *Market development:* Involves bringing current products to new markets. Usually occurs when existing markets have been fully penetrated.
- *Diversification:* Involves developing new products and bringing them into new markets. Usually implemented when no opportunities can be seen with existing products or in existing markets.

		PRODUCTS	
		Current	New
MARKETS	Current	Market Penetration	Product Development
	New	Market Development	Diversification

Figure 2. Ansoff model for growth strategies

What if growth is not the only or the most important goal of your enterprise? Indeed, organizations may implement many different strategies that fall outside the Ansoff Matrix, such as:

- *Vertical integration:* Accomplished through a firm becoming its own supplier or retailer. Usually implemented when a firm wants to secure the resources or channels needed to serve its existing market.
- *Market expansion:* Similar to market development, but more specifically seeks markets that are similar to current ones.
- *Market creation:* A new approach for businesses moving into new regional or demographic groups, where there is not a pre-existing market for a particular product and service. In this situation, a business may try to build a market through consumer education.

R. Christy, M. Karaan, and N. Wilson

- *Strategic alliances or joint ventures* refers to moving into a new market through collaboration with another firm to exchange resources and/or competencies.
- *Mergers or acquisitions*: Buying a competitor to gain its market share, access to a new market, and/or additional resources and/or competencies.

If the desired outcome is consolidation—scaling back the company's operations—businesses may opt for retrenchment, pruning, or divestment:

- *Retrenchment*: Reduction of the enterprise's commitment to existing products by withdrawal from weaker markets.
- *Pruning*: Reduction of the number of products the enterprise has in a market. Usually occurs when market segments are too small or too costly to serve.
- *Divestment*: Selling off one part of the organization to another firm and subsequently exiting a market and/or removing a product. This typically occurs when that line of business is not meeting the organization's objectives.

How Will We Get There?

After posing the questions "Who are we?" and "Where are we going?" managers must develop a plan to answer the question "How will we get there?" The answers to this question are often recorded in a formal written document called a strategic plan, which lays out the managerial process of developing and maintaining a viable fit between an organization's objectives and resources on the one hand, and its changing market opportunities on the other. The aim of the plan is to shape and reshape a company's business and products so that they combine to produce satisfactory profits and growth.

Implementation, Feedback, and Control: Making It All Happen

It may seem like your work is done once you are finished writing your strategic plan, but in fact your work is just beginning. Now that you have carefully charted your company's future, it is time to implement your plans. Even the best laid plans can fail if not implemented well. A useful tool to keep the implementation strategy on track is **project management**. Project management takes the defined goals and objectives and identifies required resources, associated budgets, and timelines for completion. Creating such a detailed implementation plan will go a long way toward success.

A key concept to remember when implementing corporate strategy is that organizations have different degrees of openness to different types of change. For example, strategies that affect the rules and culture of an organization will be met with greater resistance by staff than those that affect technology (Figure 3). This is not difficult to understand if you remember that people make up any organization, including a company. Employees will have a relatively easier time adjusting to new technology than to changes in rules and an even harder time coping with changes in the organization's culture. If you think about it, this makes sense, as culture is much more pervasive and ambiguous than a new technology or rules. It often operates on a subconscious level, too, which makes it harder to change.

Implementation has a greater chance of success if change management concepts, many of which are centered on motivating people and building a unified team, are incorporated into the implementation plan. Figure 4 lays out a variety of strategies managers can use as they plan the company's course of action, provide leadership to their team, manage operations, and track changes.

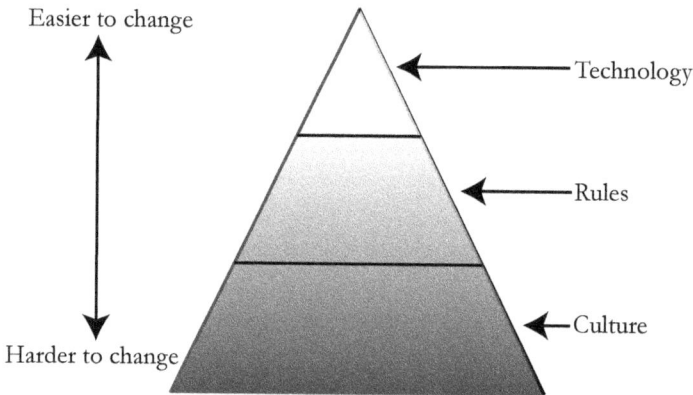

Figure 3. Levels of change

Another useful management tool is McKinsey's 7-S Model (Figure 5), which emphasizes that implementation of a new strategy requires organizational congruence with that strategy. Managers need to consider whether the people, tasks, formal organization, and informal organization (culture) each support and enable the new strategy, and if those four components support each other. Questioning these "fit" criteria will reveal elements necessary for implementation success. Does the staff have the skills required? Do daily tasks prohibit full implementation? Is the culture too

R. Christy, M. Karaan, and N. Wilson

traditional to be motivated around this innovation? Are the compensation policies motivating the desired behavior change?

Importantly, both individual and group commitment to the new plan must exist for the change strategy to be effective. Over time, the commitment level must be led by the company through these stages: awareness, understanding, positive perception, installation, adoption, and internalization.

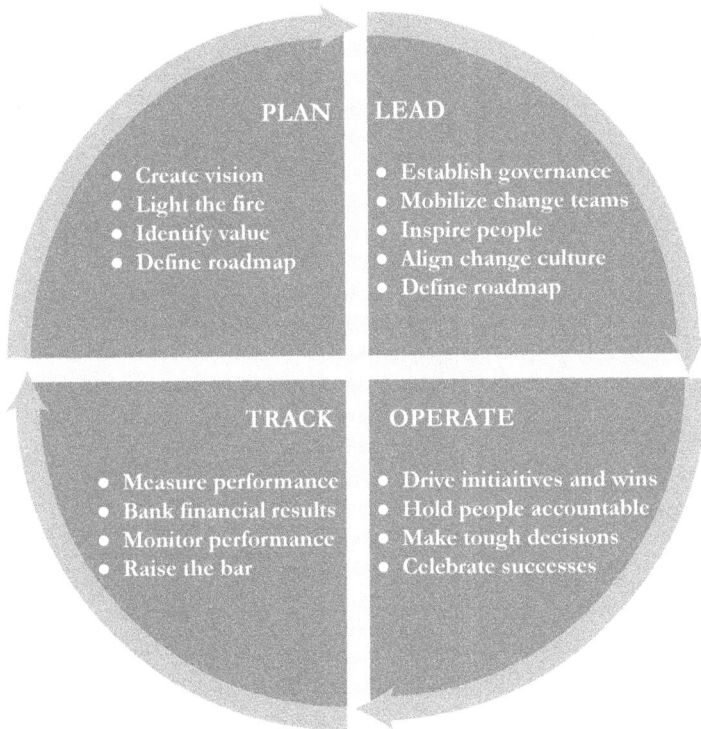

PLAN
- Create vision
- Light the fire
- Identify value
- Define roadmap

LEAD
- Establish governance
- Mobilize change teams
- Inspire people
- Align change culture
- Define roadmap

TRACK
- Measure performance
- Bank financial results
- Monitor performance
- Raise the bar

OPERATE
- Drive initiaitives and wins
- Hold people accountable
- Make tough decisions
- Celebrate successes

Figure 4: PLOT change management tool (Source: Bain & Company 2008)

Several factors are instrumental to the success of a change strategy:
- *Sponsorship*: Is there commitment to initiate the change and to sustain it later?
- *Culture*: Does the culture enable change?
- *Resistance*: Will there be strong or weak resistance among those impacted?
- *Change skills*: Does the company have the skills to manage the change process or should it seek help?
- *Leadership alignment*: Are there common goals and priorities?

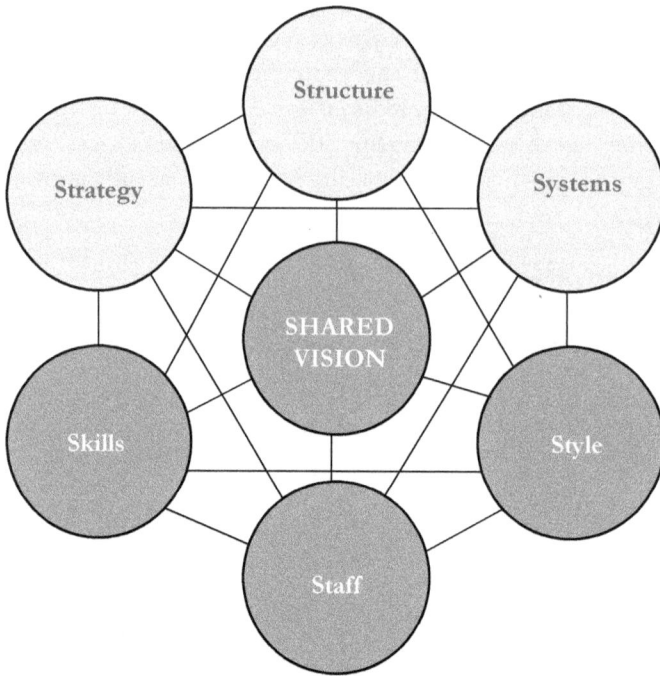

Figure 5. McKinsey 7-S Model (Source: http://www.andrewstaggs.com/the-mckinsey-7s-framework-very-useful/)

Successful change will build upon both the logical and emotional sides of change. It will also have clear sponsorship and champions at each level of the company. Other key characteristics of successful change management are a sense of urgency, a powerful coalition to initiate implementation, vision, communication, and empowerment at all levels, short-term wins, consolidation and increasing wins, and an anchor to make the change permanent.

Even with sound strategic planning and implementation, economies, governments, markets—in short, everything—can and will change. Therefore you must assess your progress periodically to see if you are moving toward success or failure. As part of your assessment you will want to revisit your mission and repeat the SWOT and PEST analyses, which in turn may lead you to revise your goals and strategies, leading to changes in implementation (Figure 6). The cyclical, feedback-based process of planning, implementing, and controlling will allow you to think in the present with an eye on the future.

R. Christy, M. Karaan, and N. Wilson

**Situation Analysis:
Who are we?**
- Mission
- Vision
- PEST

**Goals and Strategy
Identification:**
- Ansoff

**Implementation:
How do we get
there?**
- PLOT Change
- McKinsey

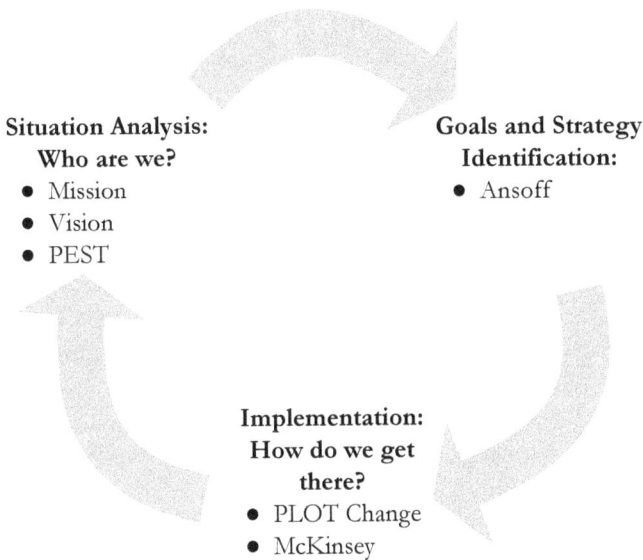

Figure 6. Overview of the strategic planning process

Best Practices in Strategic Thinking: An African Small Enterprise Perspective

Through the 15-year span of the Making Markets Matter program, we have shared these and other modern business management tools, frameworks, and principles with a wide cross-section of African SMEs along the food, fiber, and energy value chains. What we found was that entrepreneurs were eager to learn and understand the new tools, but only to the extent that they deemed them useful for their business and operations. In other words, not surprisingly, participants were primarily interested in applying the tools as opposed to merely learning about them. From our discussions we have assembled a list of 10 best practices or principles related to the implementation of strategic thinking within African SMEs.

Never major in minors. This maxim came up one day when discussing goal formulation as part of the component of strategic thinking as it relates to implementing plans. One participant was crystal clear about the role of the leader when implementing strategic thinking within a company. If goals and objectives were essential to the process, then the priority of establishing them was important as well. They must be considered in some hierarchy. Some goals are more important than others, and therefore they must be considered first when taking action. For example, if a small fire broke out in your kitchen while at the same time your roof was leaking from a pouring rain, which of those problems should you attend to first? Clearly, controlling the fire in your kitchen. But it is surprising how many people say they would go outside, get on a ladder to the roof, and fix the leak first. In short, leaders must take into consideration the importance or ranking of the goals of the organization. "Majoring in the minor problem" kills strategic thinking within our enterprises.

Bad things happen to good enterprises; keep going. With each new training program we realize just how resilient African entrepreneurs must be to operate in the less-than-perfect environment that many African economies are. Setbacks, bad breaks, and personal heartbreaks can happen to you not only as a person but also to your company: you can fall short of sale targets, employees can let you down, your competition may be unfair or dishonest. In such situations, your company should respond just like you would as a person, by acknowledging that bad things can happen to good people (enterprises), and it is not what happens but how you respond to the challenges that matters. "Just because we are a good company, we are not immune to experiencing setbacks. But when setbacks happen, we keep going."

Let the leader's intent be known. Most small business owners realize that they need to surround themselves with good employees, loyal individuals who are willing to go the extra mile to make the strategic plan work, allowing the company to reach its stated goals and objectives. In cultivating a loyal team, you, the owner or senior manager, must understand that you are also the leader of the company. As a leader, communication with employees is critical to reaching the enterprise's goals. Importantly, this includes giving employees the reasons why something must be done. Willie Pietersen (2010), South African businessman and author, expressed it this way when writing about strategic learning: "People will do almost any what, if you give them a why!"

Involve your most valuable asset—your team, your employee—in your strategic plan. For strategic plans to result in positive impacts on your company, you will need the active buy-in of your employees. Therefore, right from the beginning, ensure that they are involved in developing your mission statement, your company goals, objectives, and targets and in the creation of new products or services that chart a new direction. If you want to make sure that your strategic plans become a reality, you must involve your employees in strategic-thinking exercises; otherwise, your plans will remain dreams only.

Work on building trust. A thoughtful question can be just as important as a reasoned response to producing a powerful lesson. A memorable illustration of this happened when Strive Masiyiwa, Africa's self-made business mogul and entrepreneur, was presenting his after-dinner remarks at Making Markets Matter, and a program participant asked him, "What is your greatest constraint as an African businessman?" We were all expecting that he would point to poor infrastructure, weak legal frameworks, limited access to capital, government corruption, or another of the oft-cited "problems" with Africa. But, to our surprise, without hesitation he said that lack of trust was his biggest problem. Lack of trust? What was he talking about? Surely people trusted him, one of the most successful entrepreneurs on the continent. From his insightful remarks prompted by this thoughtful question, we knew that, for our work with the African business community to be meaningful and transformative, it would need to reach deeper than a superficial review of strategic thinking as framed in Western business discourse. We knew we had to find ways to explore with participants a more reflective understanding of the realities of operating an African business. Talking about finding ways to build trust became a key component of our discussions.

Know—and use—your mission statement. Having a good mission statement is one thing, and having that statement be well-known or even admired by your staff and employees is quite another. For a good practice, from time to time simply asks your employees "What is the mission of this company?" By doing so you are reminding them of who we are and where we are going. Of course, be sure that you first share the mission statement with them. Post it in a prominent place in your office where everyone can see it. Importantly, this practice can be employed with prospective employees as well; show them your mission statement and ask them to reflect on it.

Connect leadership and strategic thinking. Many management gurus are strong advocates of strategic thinking and planning, yet they seldom connect the importance of leadership to strategic thinking and planning. But stop for a moment to consider: How good is a strategic plan without good leadership? And conversely, how good is leadership without a plan? In fact, one may argue that Africa is one place where planning and leadership should be closely linked, as many SME owners in Africa are not only leaders in their enterprises but also in their respective communities. Leadership must be linked to strategic thinking.

Learn to live with uncertainty. Running a business is risky by nature, so entrepreneurs must be able to accept a certain level of risk. But due to a lack of enabling environments in Africa, managers operate under an even greater degree of uncertainty. Risk can be expressed in probabilistic terms. For example, the chances of your company winning a contract from a government agency is X percent. Uncertainty on the other hand has no known probable outcome; things are just uncertain, and they can turn uncertain without forewarning. Will our country experience a financial crisis or radical change in government before year's end? We do not know. Nevertheless, even under such uncertain conditions, decisions must be made. Unfortunately most business or management tools are developed under the assumption that the manager has a degree of control, and that if control is not present, then it must be acquired. This option may not be available to African enterprises.

Think about how long you want your business to live. Dr. Mohammad Karaan, then Dean of AgriSciences at Stellenbosch University in South Africa, is famous among our cast of facilitators for asking participants probing questions. On one occasion, he provoked a most memorable debate by asking entrepreneurs how long they wanted their enterprises to run. Some wanted their businesses to live only as long as they lived; others planned to pass their businesses to their children; and still others wanted their businesses to live forever. But one unusually quiet lady in the back row said that she only wanted her business "to live until it could be sold for a fortune." By acknowledging this, she revealed something important about her. She was a serial entrepreneur. Strategic thinking is often thought of as a tool that helps chart the strategic future, usually five to seven years, of a company especially during a period when a company is experiencing slowed growth. Karaan's question now requires all business leaders in Africa to entertain this issue as part of the strategic thinking process.

All markets matter. Maintaining your competitive edge is what strategic thinking is all about. Your competitiveness is linked to the market you serve. That is, a competitive business will be able to offer products and services that meet the standards of local and global markets at prices that are competitive while providing acceptable returns. What is the key take-away here? Managers in Africa must develop a mind-set that all markets matter, both local and distant ones.

Sources

Ansoff, I. (1957). Strategies for Diversification. *Harvard Business Review* 35(5): 113–124.

Gottfredson, Mark, Steve Schaubert, John Case, and Kath Tsakalakis. (2008) "Chapter Eight: The Road to Results". The Breakthrough Imperative: How the Best Managers Get Outstanding Results. HarperCollins. Books24x7. <http://common.books24x7.com.proxy.library.cornell.edu/toc.aspx?bookid=48997> (accessed April 4, 2015)

Guiltinan, J., and G. Paul (1991). Marketing Management. New York: McGraw-Hill.

Ilbury, C., and C. Sunter (2001). The Mind of a Fox. Cape Town: Human & Rousseau.

Kotler, P. (2012). Marketing Management. 14th edition. Englewood Cliffs, NJ: Prentice Hall.

Mankins, M. C., and R. Steele (2006). Stop Making Plans; Start Making Decisions. Harvard Business Review 84(1): 76–84.

Manktelow, J. (2010). The Ansoff Matrix—Understanding the Risks of Different Options. http://www.timeanalyzer.com/lib/ansoff.htm. (accessed March 10, 2015).

Pietersen, W. (2010). Strategic Learning: How to Be Smarter than Your Competition and Turn Key Insights into Competitive Advantage. Hoboken, NJ: Wiley.

Rigby, D., and B. Bilodeau (2007). Management Tools and Trends. Bain and Company.

Roxburgh, C. (2009). The Use and Abuse of Scenarios. https://www.mckinseyquarterly.com/The_use_and_abuse_of_scenarios_2463 (accessed August 23, 2010).

MARKETING STRATEGY FOR AFRICAN AGRIBUSINESSES

Edward Mabaya and Maureen Bandama

Introduction

Over the past two decades, we have had the unique privilege of working closely with many small and medium enterprises (SMEs) along the agribusiness value chains in many Africa countries. Our interaction has taken many forms including offering one-on-one business advisory services, evaluating business proposals, and through our annual executive training program, Making Markets Matter. Throughout these interactions, marketing has been raised as a key challenge facing many small farmers and agribusinesses. Indeed, with the rapid rise of supermarkets across Africa, agricultural value chains are getting increasingly formal, complex, and difficult to access. Despite all the talk about inclusive value chains, small farmers and SMEs are often faced with a reality in which there is increasing vertical integration, buyers interested only in bulk purchases (truckloads rather than a few bags), and traceability requirements too costly to implement on a small scale (Chitja and Mabaya 2015).

In this chapter we explore how marketing strategy can be used as an effective tool to reach your customers, increase profitability, and grow your business. The chapter is structured as follows. First we set the stage by defining the concept of marketing and distinguish it from selling. Next we discuss ways of dividing your market into more homogenous and manageable segments (market segmentation). Next we will help you identify the best market segments to target. For the selected market segment we discuss strategies for positioning your product using the most popular framework for designing a marketing strategy, marketing mix (product, price, place, and promotion). The chapter closes with some best practices in marketing strategy for SMEs, which we have gathered from Making Marketing Matter participants over the past 15 years.

A Market vs. Marketing vs. Selling

The terms market and marketing seem to mean different things to different people. For example, when talking about marketing, many SMEs refer to advertising, which is just one small aspect of the marketing process. In some instances marketing is taken as being synonymous with selling; the term market for many in Africa connotes an actual place, usually an open-air market for agricultural produce. Clearly it is important that we start by establishing a common understanding of marketing and markets.

In the context of this chapter, a market (the noun) can be defined as "the set of all actual and potential buyers of a product or service" or "consumers or organizations interested in a product, and with the means to buy it" (Kotler 2013). Both these definitions of market emphasize the customer's willingness and ability to purchase your product. By extension, people with neither the ability nor the willingness to purchase your product should not be considered as part of your market.

Marketing can be defined in multiple ways. The following are our favorites:

- "Marketing is the management process that identifies, anticipates and satisfies customer requirements profitably" (The Chartered Institute of Marketing 2014).
- "The right product, in the right place, at the right time, and at the right price" (Adcock et al. 2001).
- "Marketing is the social process by which individuals and groups obtain what they need and want through creating and exchanging products and value with others" (Kotler 2013).

E. Mabaya and M. Bandama

The definitions all emphasize three elements that are essential to marketing. First is the focus on the customer or client. It will be useful for you as you read through this chapter to keep your eyes on the customer. Second, all the definitions are action oriented. They emphasize a process that needs to be updated constantly to respond to both internal and external circumstances. In other words, marketing strategy is not something that you do once every few years (like strategic planning); rather it is an active process that must be managed daily. Third and last, all the definitions mention money, profits, and getting paid. Yes, indeed, marketing should be viewed as a means to an end (profitability), and therefore every aspect of marketing needs to serve the overall goal of generating profit for your business. As eloquently stated by Steven Denning (2011), "The purpose of a firm is to delight customers, at a profit."

Selling is part of the marketing process, but marketing is not just selling. These two differ fundamentally in that "selling concerns itself with the tricks and techniques of getting people to exchange their cash for your product," whereas marketing is "the entire business process [...] consisting of a tightly integrated effort to discover, create, arouse and satisfy customer needs" (Levitt 1960). To build a long lasting business, you should go beyond just getting customers to pay for your product. To survive in the long run, you should develop demand for your product and always strive to fulfill your customers' needs.

Going beyond the "Tricks": Steps to Developing a Marketing Strategy

To develop an effective marketing strategy requires both careful planning and continuous updating. Most companies use a marketing plan, which is simply a comprehensive blueprint that outlines your company's overall marketing efforts. There are three key steps to developing an effective marketing strategy: segmentation, targeting, and positioning. This is known as the STP process or target marketing. Below we expand on these key steps and follow up with a detailed discussion that includes some useful tools.

Segmentation simply refers to ways to divide the market into groups according to various criteria that are likely to influence consumer behaviors and patterns. For example, you can divide the market by geography (urban vs. rural consumers), age (young vs. old people), gender (women vs. men), etc.

Targeting is the process of selecting one (or a few) of the market segments that will be your primary focus. When selecting a market segment, you want to look for "attractiveness" and "fit." An attractive market segment is one that is growing and has relatively few competitors. Be sure to think about whether the segment is a good fit for your company. For example, can your company produce enough for the particular segment? Can you compete with already existing companies?

Positioning refers to all aspects of engaging your customer in the market and distinguishing yourself from your competitors. Where do you advertise and display your product? You can use the marketing mix (product, place, price and promotion) to position your product.

Segmenting a Market

Segmentation variables are characteristics of individuals, groups, or organizations that are used to divide a market into smaller and more homogenous groups or segments. There are two key approaches to segmenting consumer markets—consumer characteristics and consumer responses.

Consumer Characteristics

Geographic: Geographic variables are those that are related to the geographic location of the consumer. They include climate, terrain, city size, and urban or rural areas. If your product is bulky, as is often the case with agricultural products, it makes sense to segment your market by geography.

Demographic: The most commonly used demographic variables include age, gender, ethnicity, income, education, occupation, family size, religion, and social class. With the possible exception of cosmetic products, we caution against using race as a way to segment a market because it masks the true underlying demographic variables.

Psychographic: Psychographic segmentation divides consumers into groups based on their lifestyle and personality, such as values, attitudes, and opinions. For example, there is a growing movement toward organic, earth-friendly, or sustainably harvested products.

Consumer Responses

Occasion: You can segment consumers based on the occasion for which they use your product. For example, some consumers buy wine for special occasions, while others buy it for everyday use.

Benefits: You can segment consumers based on the benefits that they seek from a product or service. This is especially helpful when the product has multiple uses.

Usage: You can segment consumers based on their usage of a product or service. First you can segment the market into users and nonusers, and then further segment the users into heavy, moderate, and light users.

Attitudes: This segmentation asks what is the attitude of the consumer toward the product?" Consumers can be segmented into enthusiastic, positive, indifferent, negative, and hostile toward the product (Kotler 2013).

A simple way to segment your market is to pick two segregation variables that are suitable to your product or service. You can then put the different classes of each variable onto a grid with one variable on the vertical axis and another variable on the horizontal axis. Each of the resulting boxes becomes a separate market segment. Whatever variables you choose to use in segmenting your market should result in segments that are measurable, accessible, actionable, and suitable for your company.

Targeting

Once you have segmented the market, you need to set priorities about which consumer groups or segments you will target first—this is what targeting is all about. How do you evaluate the attractiveness of a market segment? You can look at the following characteristics: size of segment, growth potential of segment, profitability of segment, and the segment's fit with your company's goals, mission, and core competencies. A commonly used framework for evaluating the attractiveness of a market segment is Porter's (1979) five forces model illustrated in Figure 1. Here is a quick look at each of these five forces.

Industry competitors: A segment is unattractive if the industry contains strong aggressive competitors, who will likely engage in price wars and advertising battles.

Potential entrants: A segment is unattractive if new competitors can easily enter.

Threat of substitutes: A segment is unattractive if there exist actual or potential substitutes of your product.

Supplier power: A segment is unattractive if suppliers have power. This may increase the price of inputs.

Buyer power: A segment is unattractive if the buyer has power. This forces the price of your products down, thereby undercutting profits.

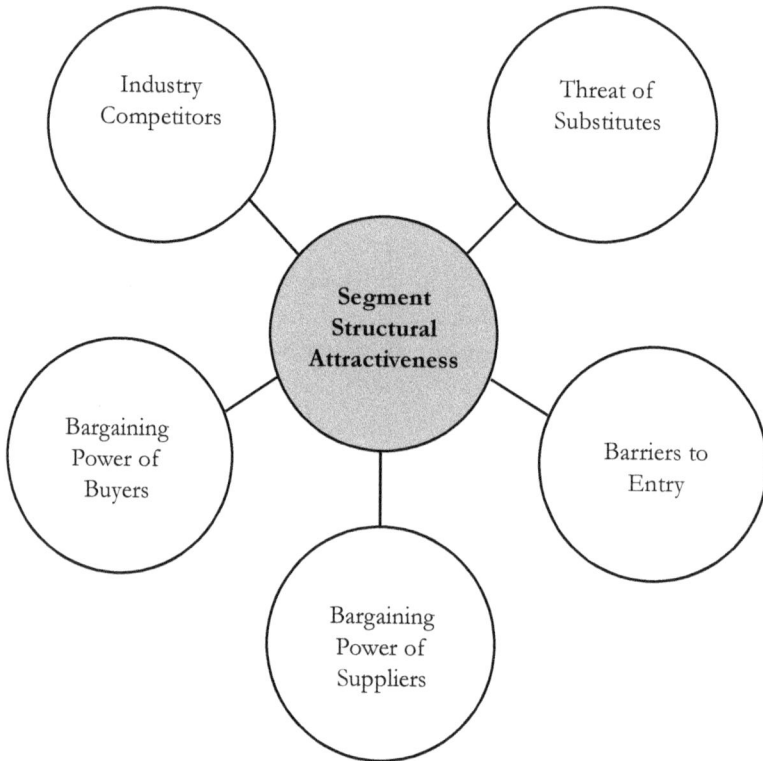

Figure 1. Porter's Five Forces model of segment attractiveness

Market Positioning

The final part of the STP process, positioning, is the act of designing your company and its products to appeal to the customer against your competitors. You may also think of it as a way of identifying a market niche for your

E. *Mabaya and M. Bandama*

brand. There are many ways to position a product in the market. Here we choose to use "marketing mix" to position our product in the market. Marketing mix is probably the most popular framework for designing a marketing strategy. Also known as the four P's, the marketing mix elements are price, place, product, and promotion (Figure 2). It is a set of tools firms use to pursue their marketing objectives in the target market (Kotler 2013).

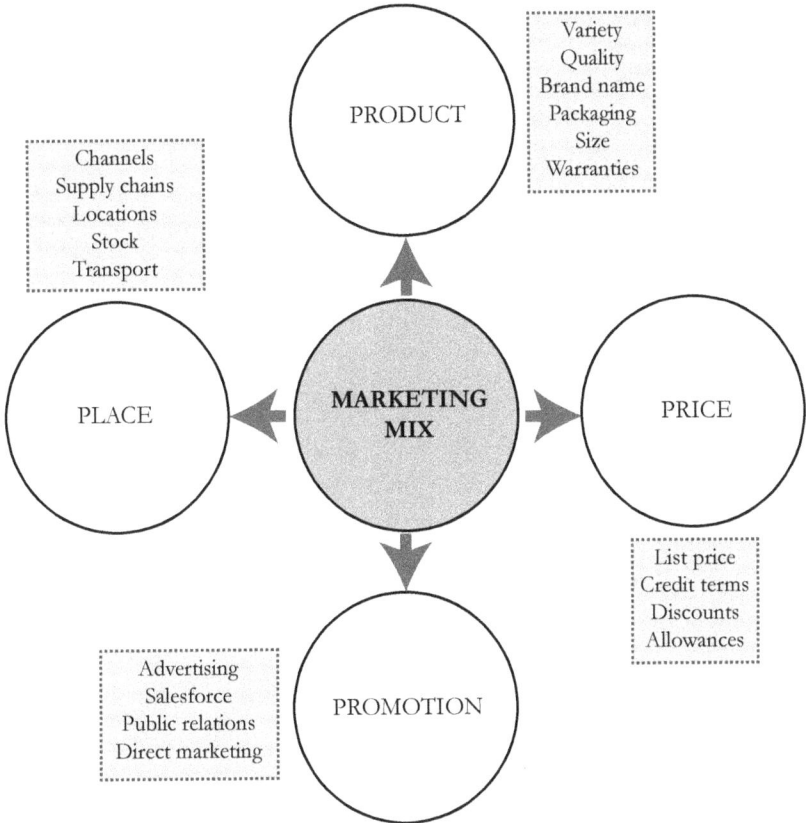

Figure 2. The Marketing Mix

It is important to understand that the various components of the marketing mix have to be well coordinated to formulate a successful marketing strategy. You may think of the marketing mix as the various ingredients that it takes to make a good stew. You need good meat, water, oil, and salt as the critical ingredients. But you can also add onions, tomatoes, curry, bay leaf, mushrooms, etc., depending on your taste. Most importantly, the ingredients are not as important as having the right mix. You need all the components to be well balanced as one unified recipe - the marketing strategy. Note that the marketing mix elements are formulated as viewed by the marketing manager and not by the customer. Each of the elements (four P's) is associated with a C from the consumer's point of view as follows (Needham 1996):

Four P's	Four C's
Product	Customer solution
Price	Customer cost
Place	Convenience
Promotion	Communication

Product—More than Meets the Eye

Of the marketing mix elements, let's start with product since this is probably what you know the most about. A product is a good, a service, or an idea that can be offered to a market to satisfy a want or need (Kotler 2000). Let's look at two key frameworks that are useful in understanding your product—the product life cycle and the three levels of a product.

The Product Life Cycle

The product life cycle assumes that every product will go through four key phases, namely, introduction, growth, maturity, and decline. Because of the nature of competition in each phase, the marketing strategy has to be adjusted accordingly. Figure 3 illustrates the typical product life cycle. Let's explore each of these phases in turn.

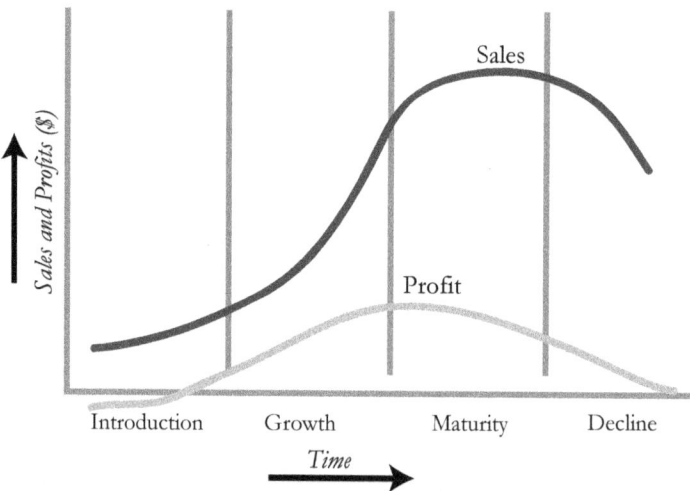

Figure 3. The Product Life Cycle

Introduction: A subsequent chapter on new product development discusses in detail the processes involved in new product development. When all of the research and development has taken place, a product is introduced to the market. The emphasis during this phase is to create awareness and appreciation of the product. Sales are likely to be low and most products will make a loss in this phase. Discounted prices are useful in inducing trial. Note that many products never make it past this first phase. Price and promotion are the key elements that can be adjusted in this introductory phase.

Growth: Assuming that your product makes it past the introductory phase, sales will start to increase as awareness of the product increases. This is the honeymoon phase. As sales increase, so do profits. Unfortunately, all this success also attracts competition. Your focus in this phase should be to keep ahead of your competitors. You can do this by extending your coverage and shifting the promotion message from awareness to preference. You will need to adjust your prices as you benchmark your competitors.

Maturity: As with human and other life forms, products that survive the earlier phases tend to spend the longest time in the maturity phase. As a product matures, sales grow at a decreasing rate and then stabilize. With so many products in the market, producers try to differentiate their products from the competition. Price competition intensifies, which lowers profitability. A key strategy for the maturity phase is to build and maintain customer loyalty through innovative promotion strategies. Your goal is to extend this phase for as long as you can.

Decline: Unfortunately, this phase is often the beginning of the end. The main trigger of the decline phase is that newer, better, or more innovative products have entered the market. For example, the entry of digital cameras resulted in a decline for film sales and photo processing. Changes in consumer preferences can also push your product into the decline phase. This is why it is important for your company to keep an eye on consumer trends. You can still extend the life of your product by lowering prices and cutting production and marketing costs.

Three Levels of a Product

Another useful concept that will help you rethink your company's product is to realize that every product has three layers as illustrated in Figure 4. The core product is the benefit or service that the product delivers to the consumer. The tangible product is the physical product that you can touch, see, and smell. The augmented product is an extra or bonus feature that comes with your product. Let's take the example of a company that sells eggs. The core product in this case is good health and nutrition. The tangible product is one dozen eggs in a paper or plastic crate. To augment the product you could add recipes, nutritional facts, use before date, and other information on the packaging. We are sure you have given some thought to improving your tangible product. To keep a competitive edge in the market, you need to constantly find innovative ways to improve all three levels of your product.

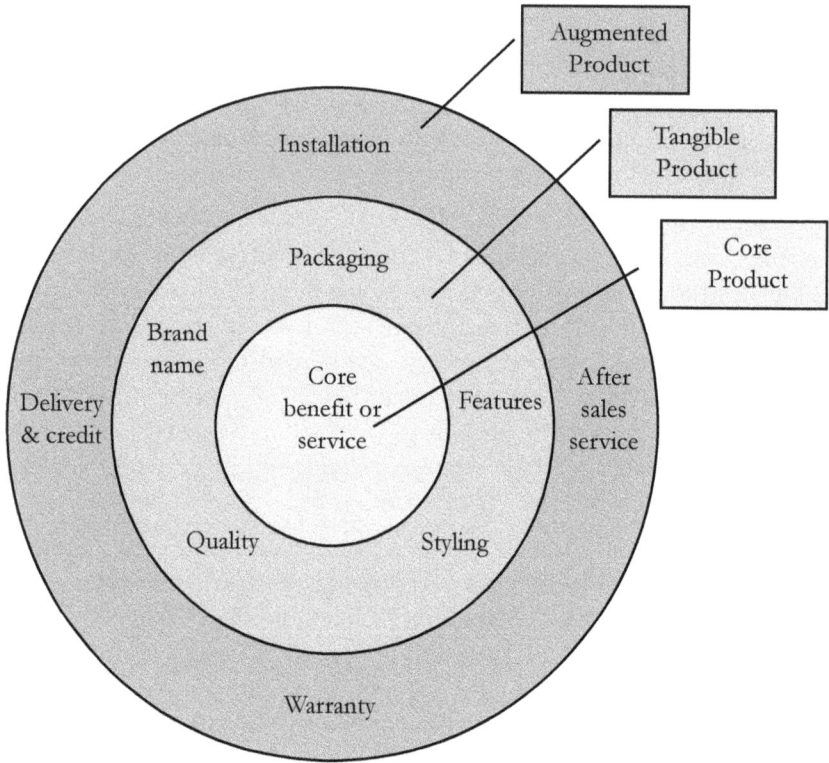

Figure 4. Three levels of a product (Source: Kotler, 2000)

Pricing—How Much Is Too Much?

When you are budgeting for your marketing activities, keep in mind that price is the only variable of the marketing mix that generates revenue. All the other variables of the four P's contribute to costs for the firm. A company maximizing profits will thus focus on pricing. Also keep in mind that, unlike in the past, today consumers have great access to information (e.g., through mobile phone and the internet). This makes it easier for consumers to gather price information about competing products at minimal search costs. The area of competition for a company is thus expanded. Also note that prices are easy to change compared with the other three P's. There is little or no cost to changing prices. It is thus an easy short-term strategy.

There are many ways to price a product. Here we look at some of them and try to understand the best policy/strategy in various situations. Depending on the quality of a product, you may consider four key pricing strategies as illustrated in Figure 5.

	Low Price	**High Price**
Low Quality	Economy	Skimming
High Quality	Penetration	Premium

Figure 5. The four key pricing strategies

Premium pricing: It often costs more to produce high-quality products. To be profitable, these high-quality products have to be sold at a high price. Fortunately consumers, especially those in high-income segments, are willing to pay premium price for superior quality. For example, in most African markets, green-bottle beers (often import brands such as Amstel, Heineken, and Peroni) are sold at a premium price compared with brown-bottle beers.

Penetration pricing: While the products are still high quality, the price charged for products and services is set relatively low in order to penetrate the market. Once this is achieved, the price is increased. A seed company trying to introduce a new variety to the market may offer a discounted price for the variety as part of penetration pricing. This will induce trial and the seed company can always increase prices in subsequent years. It is important to at least signal a higher price to come by indicating that this is a special introductory price.

Economy pricing: This is a no-frills low price that often comes with low-quality products. The cost of marketing and manufacturing are kept at a minimum. For example, the no-name brand baked beans that you can buy at your local supermarket probably utilizes economy pricing. Because of the low purchasing power of most consumers in Africa, this pricing strategy is effective in reaching "the bottom of the pyramid" (Prahalad 2009.

Skimming: This pricing strategy occurs when you charge a high price for a poor-quality product because you have a substantial competitive advantage. The advantage is not sustainable, however, because the high price tends to attract new competitors into the market, and the price inevitably has to fall due to increased supply. In a market where quality is not obvious, e.g., wine or cheese, some companies use high prices to mislead consumers into thinking that the product is of higher quality.

Beyond the four key pricing strategies, there are many pricing strategies that you can use in different situations. For example, you can choose to undercut your competitor with predatory pricing or you can engage in discriminatory pricing by charging different prices to different market segments for the same product. Psychological pricing such as charging $9.99 instead of $10.00 is designed to have a positive psychological impact on the buyer.

Place—Getting Your Product to the Consumer

Another element of the marketing mix is place. Place is also commonly referred to as channel, distribution, supply chain, or intermediary. It is the mechanism through which products are moved from the manufacturer to the end consumer. Figure 6 shows a typical distribution channel for agricultural produce in many African countries.

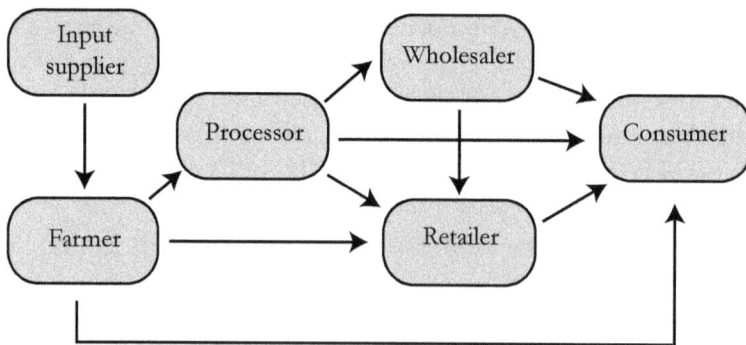

Figure 6. A typical supply chain for agricultural products

As a manufacturer or producer of a product, you have to keep in mind six basic place decisions.

1. Do we use direct or indirect channels? For example in a farmer's market, the product goes directly from farmer to consumer, whereas wholesalers are an example of indirect channels.
2. Do you use single or multiple channels? For a small enterprise it may be cheaper to start off with only one channel and then expand to other channels as your market grows.
3. How long does it take for your product to reach the consumer? This aspect is especially important for agricultural products that are highly perishable.
4. What types of intermediary do you use? The type of intermediary used can determine sales margins as well as ownership of a product.
5. What is the number of intermediaries at each level? Depending on the market segments selected, you need to decide on the optimal number of intermediaries at each level of the supply chain.
6. Which companies are likely to result in intrachannel conflict? Intrachannel conflict is the infighting that can result from having several different businesses along the supply chain. For example, there may be some retailer that demands exclusivity as part of the conditions for stocking your product.

As an SME, your enterprise will have to be creative in creating distribution channels that are affordable and effective in reaching your customers. For example, Wild Fruits of Africa, a small food manufacturer based in Botswana that specializes in snacks made from indigenous fruits, has collaborated with the national airline (Air Botswana) to distribute small samples of its product to passengers (Mabaya et al. 2014). On the backside of these airline samples is information on where one can buy more products.

Promotion—Getting the Message Out

Another key element of the marketing mix is promotion. Promotion includes all of the tools available to the marketer for marketing communication. Marketing communications has its own promotions mix. Elements of the promotions mix are integrated to form a coherent campaign. As with all forms of communication, the message from the marketer follows the communications process. Below we elaborate on some individual components of the promotions mix that might be relevant for your business.

Personal selling is an effective way to manage personal customer relationships. In personal selling, salespersons act on behalf of your business. They are usually well trained in the approaches and techniques of personal selling. Salespeople are very expensive, however, and should be used only when there is a genuine return on investment. They may not be a viable option for most start-ups.

Sales promotion refers to all promotions other than advertising, personal selling, and public relations. A good example of sales promotion is the BOGOF, or buy-one-get-one-free, promotion. You can also use coupons, competitions, and introductory offers. To get the best bang for you money, keep track of how much each promotion costs and weigh this against the increase in sales revenue.

Trade fairs and exhibitions are good for making new contacts and renewing old ones. Although companies seldom sell much at such events, the purpose is to network, increase awareness, and induce trial. Examples of such platforms include the annual agricultural shows held in most Southern African countries, such as the Zambia Agricultural and Commercial Show. Another platform that is becoming increasingly more popular is weekend farmers' markets, where farmers can interact directly with the consumer.

Advertising is a communication that you pay for. It develops attitudes, creates awareness, and transmits information to the consumer. There are many advertising media such as newspapers, magazines and journals, television, in-store posters, and outdoor billboards.

Word of mouth, though passive on the side of the business, presents the most effective way to communicate to your customer. By delivering a superb service, businesses can build a good reputation and positively manage their public image. For example, farmers who are happy with a new seed variety are likely to recommend it to their neighbors.

Sponsorship refers to organizations paying to be associated with a particular event, cause, or image. Companies sponsor sports events such as the local football team. The goodwill attributes of the event are then associated with the sponsoring organization.

Top Ten Lessons on Marketing

We close this chapter by sharing some key lessons in marketing, which we have learned from African agribusinesses we have met through Making Markets Matter. You can think of these as best practices from your colleagues and we hope that some of them will be useful as you develop an effective marketing strategy for your enterprise.

1. *Promotion costs money; not advertising costs more.* The days when good work simply spoke for itself are no more. Your customers are bombarded with images and information on various products, and before your product can speak for itself, it has to be given a chance, a platform to do so. This is where promotion comes in by directing the customer's focus to your product, so that it may have a chance to "speak" its quality attributes to the consumer in the face of fierce competition from other products. Yes, this will cost some money, but you should consider the loss in sales that can result from not promoting your product.

2. *Incentives for your sales team matter.* Your sales team most often represents the face of the business and their interactions with your customers can make or break your business. The business reputation not only lies in customer satisfaction with the actual product, but with the "service" received in obtaining the product. Incentives for your sales teams give them the added oomph to provide the best possible service. The incentives do not always have to be financial. For example, Suba Agro, a seed company in Tanzania, awards its best salesperson each year with a bursary to attend Making Markets Matter.

3. *Be accessible to your customers.* Create a platform to interface with your customers away from the shop floor or marketplace. Here you will be able to communicate to clients facts about your products and developments within your business, and they in turn are able to communicate with you about your product and their needs. Have an online presence like a website, Facebook page, or Twitter account for the business and communicate your e-mail address and cell phone number. Let your customers know all the ways in which they are able to access you and your business.

4. *Pick up the low-hanging fruits.* As a small agribusiness enterprise, you are well positioned to take advantage of the efforts of local governments and nongovernmental organizations (NGOs) in fostering SMEs. Be in the know, keep yourself up to date and informed of all the opportunities governments and NGOs offer that can be of benefit to you and your

business. Many governments and NGOs are involved in improving performance of small businesses, linking them with technology, finance, and expertise. At times governments and NGOs present a good frontier for markets through their procurement policies and strategies. For long-term survival, however, do not depend too heavily on such contracts, as they are unreliable.

5. *Word of mouth is the best form of advertising.* Best of all, word of mouth is free—except, of course, for the fact that you have to build a good reputation by providing a great product and excellent service. When your customers are happy with your product, they will tell everybody and recommend it. The same is also true when they are unhappy with your product or service. In the age of online technology, word of mouth has a far greater reach than ever before as it is no longer limited to the people your customer actually sees. A good word about your businesses posted on Facebook, WhatsApp, or Twitter has a wide reach. Potential customers often reach out into their networks for recommendations on which products to use or try out and which ones to avoid. Customer recommendations and comments on your website or Facebook page also present a frontier for word of mouth advertising.

6. *If you can't beat them, join them.* As a small business, you may be tempted to look at everyone as your competition, especially in the marketing arena. Upon closer inspection, however, you will notice that there are a lot of opportunities in partnering with others. Instead of fighting to get a bigger slice of the cake, small businesses can work together to grow the cake for mutual benefit. We have witnessed many SME seed companies doing business together for mutual benefit.

7. *Measure the effectiveness of all marketing efforts.* Since you are going to spend time and money on it, and the viability of your business is intrinsically linked to it, an evaluation of your marketing efforts is an absolute necessity. When you have planned and implemented your marketing efforts, find out which are most effective and which are less so and adjust your efforts accordingly bearing in mind that the market is always changing.

8. *Marketing is communicating.* Information such as the product's price, if the product is on promotion and for how long, quality or attribute information is important to the customer. For example, a sign promoting "grain fed eggs for sale" provides more information to the customer than just "eggs." The more information you can share with the customer

about benefits and proper use of your product, the more likely you are to build a loyal customer base. You should also consider labeling your product in local languages, as this not only helps in communicating your message but also builds a "home grown" perception of your product.

9. *Copy other businesses and learn from their mistakes.* In the world of business, originality is overrated. Your business does not have to reinvent the wheel. Instead, you can lower your risks significantly buy learning from others. If you see a packaging or promotional strategy from your competitors that seems to be working well, you can copy the strategy and perhaps improve on it. Just be sure to respect copyrights.

10. *Know your costumers.* Marketing is a process rather than an event or task. Therefore marketing strategies, plans, and activities should be frequently reviewed and renewed, as market conditions are never static. Make it a point to talk to some customers every week. Keeping an ongoing conversation with your customers is the only way you can stay ahead of the competition. If you have business partners such as distributors or suppliers, you should invest time in understanding their strategic plans and how these might affect your business.

Sources

Adcock, D., A. Halborg, and C. Ross (2001). *Introduction Marketing: Principles and Practice* (4th ed.). Harlow: Pearson Education.

The Chartered Institute of Marketing (2007). *Shape the Agenda. Tomorrow's World. Re-evaluating the Role of Marketing.* Berkshire: The Chartered Institute of Marketing Publications.

The Chartered Institute of Marketing. (2014). Marketing Planning Tool http://www.cim.co.uk/marketingplanningtool/intro.asp#bookmark2 (accessed November 20, 2014).

Chitja, J. and E. Mabaya (2015). Institutional Innovations Linking Small-Scale Produce Farmers to Markets in South Africa. *In* R. D. Christy, C. A. da Silva, N. Mhlanga, K. Tihanyi, and E. Mabaya (eds.), *Innovative Institutions, Public Policies, and Private Strategies for Agro-Enterprise Development* (1–24). Singapore: World Scientific Publishing.

Denning, Steve. (2011). Is Delighting the Customer Profitable? *Forbes* (April 1).

Kotler, P. (2000). *Marketing Management: Millennium Edition.* New Jersey: Prentice Hall.

Kotler, P. (2013). *Principles of Marketing.* New Jersey: Prentice Hall.

Levitt, Theodore (1960). Marketing myopia. *Harvard Business Review* 38(4): 24–47.

Mabaya, E., J. Jackson, G. Ruethling, C. M. Carter, and J. Castle (2014). Wild Fruits of Africa: Commercializing Natural Products to Improve Rural Livelihoods in Southern Africa. *International Food and Agribusiness Management Review (IFAMR), Special Issue: African Agribusiness on the Move* 17(B): 69–74.

Needham, Dave (1996). *Business for Higher Awards*. Oxford, England: Heinemann.

Porter, Michael E. (1979). How Competitive Forces Shape Strategy. *Harvard Business Review* (March): 21–38.

Prahalad, Coimbatore Krishna (2009). *The fortune at the bottom of the pyramid, revised and updated 5th anniversary edition: Eradicating poverty through profits*. New Jersey: FT Press.

CASH FLOW MANAGEMENT IN AFRICAN AGRIBUSINESSES

Onkutlwile Othata

Introduction

Experts agree that many businesses fail because of poor management and, more specifically, pinpoint poor cash flow management—the practice of controlling the movement of liquid cash in and out of the organization—as the main reason. For small businesses in particular, the ability to manage cash flows is crucial (Ebben and Johnson 2011). As a long-time facilitator of the Making Markets Matter agribusiness training program, I have heard many small and medium enterprise (SME) owners and managers lament that cash flow management is a daunting task. The reality is that it is a fairly easy task, but, like any other important aspect of business management, it requires the combined efforts of key people in the organization and the attention of top management. Contrary to what small business owners may think, this by no means implies that all concerned personnel necessarily have to be experts in accountancy or finance. As this chapter demonstrates, a clear understanding of the organization and its business cycle is crucial, whereas a basic understanding of accountancy is at best an added advantage. The chapter starts with an overview of cash flow management, then discusses the different components of the practice followed by a discussion of the cash budget before looking at some strategies for dealing with cash deficits and cash surpluses. The chapter then offers insights into best practices for African SMEs and concludes with a summary.

Overview of Cash Flow Management

Cash flow management is about planning to receive and spend cash. It starts with a forecast of how much money the company will receive and how much it will spend to make its payments. The forecast is dependent mainly on in-depth knowledge of customers, suppliers, and operations. Once the forecast is complete, financial managers compare receipts and payments to determine whether the business will have the cash needed to meet its expenses and obligations; in other words, is the business likely to have a cash surplus or shortage? If forecasts indicate a shortage or deficit, management needs to explore strategies to rectify the situation. If, on the other hand, the forecast shows a surplus, management can explore different avenues of investing or spending the surplus cash. All these steps are explained in greater detail below.

Cash Flow Forecasting

A forecast is nothing but an estimate, and therefore, in estimating cash flows, it is advisable to follow the accountancy principle of "conservatism." Simply put, this means that one would rather be pessimistic than optimistic—rather underestimate revenues and overestimate expenses. For example, if in the past receipts have ranged between $10,000 and $20,000, it is best to use a figure closer to $10,000 in forecasting revenues. For expenses, on the other hand, the figure to use should be closer to the higher end of the historical range.

It is also important that the estimates are as close to "reality" as possible. For businesses that have been in operation, past data are often a good source, but for start-ups, a lot depends on management's ability to come up with realistic estimates based on industry information and other statistics. Either way, knowledge of customers, suppliers, and operations is still key. Knowledge of customers enables management to know how much cash to expect from customers and when. Similarly, knowledge of suppliers and operations enables management to know how much has to be paid out and when. Knowledge about customers, suppliers, and operations helps management answer two sets of key questions:

O. Othata

- Is the business likely to run short of cash? If so, when? Most importantly, when this happens, what is our plan to pay for liabilities and other obligations?
- Is the business likely to have excess or surplus cash? If so, when? Most importantly, when this happens, how do we plan to use the extra cash?

These questions are the cornerstone of cash flow management.

Knowing and Understanding Our Customers

All businesses generate cash by supplying goods or services to customers, so it is important that management knows and understands customers. We want to know how much they consume and, perhaps most importantly, their paying habits and the extent to which they can be influenced to pay on time. Data from international sources such as the Credit Management Research Centre indicate that many companies take, on average, 44 to 58 days to pay, despite the generally accepted payment period of 30 days. Some international companies reportedly take more than 200 days to pay—almost seven months. For many small businesses, going without payments for seven months could mean bankruptcy and closure. Furthermore, the longer a debt stays unpaid, the more likely it will become a bad debt. All this underscores the importance of knowing and understanding customers.

Typically customers can be classified into one of four categories. Let us take a look at these categories in detail.

Type 1: Powerful Customers

Customers who fall into this category typically bring substantial business to the company and are often not easy to influence. In fact, they often dictate the terms of business including terms of payment and quantities. They buy mainly on credit and prefer to pay after weeks or even months. Often they exceed the agreed credit period. Powerful customers rarely default, but they are notorious for paying late. They include government departments, big chain stores, and international companies; they also include financial service providers, though the latter tend to pay on time. Many African agribusiness SMEs prefer to do business with these types of customers if only because they are guaranteed bulk sales.

The challenge with powerful customers is that their tendency to pay late can lead to serious short-term cash shortages for your company. Because they buy in large quantities, these short-term cash shortages can be substantial enough to lead to major problems for your business, such as failure to pay suppliers and employees, which in turn can stop production. Because not much can be done to force this type of customer to pay on time, the best mitigation strategy for management is to focus on controlling cash outflows (that is, payments to suppliers and for other expenses) as much as possible to avoid cash shortages.

Type 2: Not-So-Powerful Customers ("Pretenders")

Customers who fall into this category also bring substantial business to your company and they may at first appear to be powerful customers. In fact, many of them are big local stores, chain stores, and international companies, just like your powerful customers. But beware! They also like to buy on credit and dictate credit terms, but, unlike with powerful customers, there is no guarantee of full payment with this customer type. Further, they are fond of negotiating discounts, disputing amounts, quantities, and paying late. Because they may be difficult to distinguish from powerful customers, your company may fall prey to them. But once they are identified, you may be able to influence them because generally they are not in the good books of many. They account for a fair amount of bad debts. Not-so-powerful customers exert pressure on your cash flow, and your best bet is to actively manage sales to them as well as payments.

Type 3: Loyal Customers

Customers in this category are typically smaller and often have a limited choice of organizations to buy from. They purchase smaller quantities both on cash and credit basis. Though at times they may struggle to pay on time, they are honest and transparent in doing business, and may be influenced to pay on time. They are easy to identify and individually exert less pressure on cash inflows. A useful strategy to manage them may be to offer payment incentives such as an early payment discount. Loyal customers account for a very small amount of bad debts.

Type 4: Anonymous Customers

Customers in this category buy small quantities on a cash basis and pose very little threat to cash inflows. The major problem is that they have erratic buying patterns and therefore it may be difficult for you to forecast how much to expect from them. The positive is that they pay on the spot, however, and hence never need to be chased to make payment. If all your customers fall into this category, you need to do little in terms of managing cash inflows.

Anonymous customers are common for many African agribusiness SMEs that sell their produce at the farm or production site.

Impact of Different Customers on Cash Inflows

Let us illustrate the impact of different types of customers on cash inflows through a case analysis of Foodpress Ltd., a hypothetical new food processing company. Initial forecasts estimate that Foodpress will be able to sell at least $150,000 worth of produce in each of its first three months. At first glance, this may appear to indicate that the company expects to receive $150,000 each month, but this is not necessarily the case. How much the company can expect to receive depends on the types of customers it has and their payment terms. To illustrate the point, let us consider three simple scenarios.

Scenario 1: All Customers are Anonymous (Type 4)

In this case all customers buy on a cash basis, so the company will have collected the entire $150,000 cash at the end of each of the three months. Table 1 summarizes the receipts pattern.

Table 1. Cash sales receipts

	January	February	March
Receipts	$150,000	$150,000	$150,000

Table 1 indicates that since everybody buys on a cash basis, cash receipts are expected to stay unchanged through the months January to March. But this scenario is unlikely to apply to the majority of agribusiness SMEs that either buy their supplies from farms or source from own small farms and sell them in open African markets. A more likely scenario is that the SME will have more than one type of customers and that some of them will buy on credit as opposed to on cash basis only. Scenario 2 demonstrates the impact of having customers who buy on credit.

Scenario 2. All customers are powerful (Type 1)

If all customers are powerful customers and the credit terms are that 50% be paid by the end of the first month, 30% by the end of the second month, and the balance by the end of the third month, the cash receipt pattern from sales made in January will be as follows:

January:	(50% of $150,000)	$75,000
February:	(30% of $150,000)	$45,000
March:	(balance)	$30,000

The cash receipt pattern from sales made in February will be as follows

February:	(50% of $150,000)	$75,000
March:	(30% of $150,000)	$45,000
April:	(balance)	$30,000

The cash receipt pattern from sales made in March will be as follows

March:	(50% of $150,000)	$75,000
April:	(30% of $150,000)	$45,000
May:	(balance)	$30,000

The total cash available to the firm in its first three months is summed up in Table 2, which indicates that in January, February, and March the company expects to receive $75,000, $120,000, and $150,000, respectively. These amounts differ from those illustrated in Table 1 simply because of the different type of customer and payment terms assumed.

Table 2. Receipts pattern from Type 1 customer

	January	February	March
Cash from January sales	75,000	45,000	30,000
Cash from February sales		75,000	45,000
Cash from March sales			75,000
Total	**75,000**	**120,000**	**150,000**

A comparison of Table 1 and Table 2 clearly demonstrates the impact that different customer types and payment terms have on cash flows. To further buttress this point, scenario 3 illustrates another possible cash flow stream when the company has different types of customers.

Scenario 3: Mixed Customer Types
Still assuming the total sales to be $150,000, let 50% of these be to Type 1 Customers (that is, $75,000), 30% be to Type 2 Customers (that is, $45,000) and the remaining 20% (that is, $30,000) to Type 3 Customers. Payment terms for the three types of Customers are as follows:

Type 1 Customers pay 50% at the end of the month, 30% at the end of the following month, 20% at the end of the third month, thus paying off 100% of the money owed.

Type 2 Customers pay the entire amount 30 days after sale. However, market information indicates that, in general, these Customers pay 90-95% of their debts, and the rest ends up as bad debt. Following our prudence principle, we assume the worst case scenario and estimate to collect only 90% of the $45,000, or $40,500 at the end of the second month.

Type 3 Customers pay 40% at the end of the first month, 60% at the end of the following month, thus paying off 100% of the money owed. Table 3 summarizes these receipt patterns.

Table 3. Receipts pattern from sales to three customer types

	January	February	March
Receipts from Type 1			
Cash from January sales	$37,500	$22,500	$15,000
Cash from February sales	—	37,500	22,500
Cash from March sales	—	—	37,500
Total from Type 1	**37,500**	**60,000**	**75,000**
Receipts from Type 2			
Cash from January sales	0	40,500	0
Cash from February sales	—	0	40,500
Cash from March sales	—	—	0
Total from Type 2	**0**	**40,500**	**40,500**
Receipts from Type 3			
Cash from January sales	12,000	18,000	
Cash from February sales		12,000	18,000
Cash from March sales			12,000
Total from Type 3	**12,000**	**30,000**	**30,000**
Total receipts	**$49,500**	**$130,500**	**$145,500**

Knowing and Understanding Suppliers

Suppliers are just as important as customers because they determine how much your company has to pay out and by when. Therefore, to the extent possible, you should negotiate the purchase, delivery, and payment terms with your suppliers. Typically suppliers are one of three types.

Type 1: Powerful Suppliers

Like powerful customers, powerful suppliers by and large supply on their own terms and also dictate payment terms. Powerful suppliers are reliable and supply the right quantity and quality on time. Examples include international companies, large local wholesalers, and chain stores. They prefer to deal with organizations that meet their payment terms, so they do exert pressure for payments to be made within 30 days. If their terms are not met, they may well suspend supply until they have been paid. It is thus problematic to delay paying them.

Type 2: Small Suppliers

The small supplier is the opposite of the powerful supplier. The small supplier is the "term taker" and hence easy to influence. The small supplier is more willing to allow you the payment and delivery terms that you prefer. Small suppliers seldom suspend supply if they have not been paid mainly because few companies are prepared to do business with them. It is thus easier to delay paying them. Examples include small, local shops and small (usually subsistence) farmers who supply small quantities of vegetables, fruits, and livestock directly from the farms.

Type 3: Average Suppliers

The average supplier sits somewhere between powerful and small suppliers. Examples include medium-sized semicommercial farmers and local supermarkets. This type often has an equal footing in negotiations of payment terms and exerts a fair amount of pressure on cash flows.

Impact of Different Suppliers on Cash Flows

As with customers, the impact of different types of suppliers on cash outflows is best demonstrated through an example. Continuing with the example of Foodpress Ltd. above, the forecast purchases for each of the first three months of the year are $60,000. As already explained in the case of sales, this does not necessarily mean that the company has to pay $60,000 for purchases each month. How much the company has to pay will depend on the types of suppliers it has. Scenarios 1 and 2 below help illustrate this.

Scenario 1.

Let 60% of purchases be from powerful suppliers, which are strict on being paid after one month, and the remainder from small suppliers, which are happy to receive 50% after 30 days and the rest after 60 days. The payment pattern is depicted in Table 4.

Scenario 2.

Let 60% of purchases be from powerful suppliers that want to be paid 60% during the month and the rest a month later; 40% of purchases from average suppliers that have agreed to be paid after one month. Table 5 summarizes the payment patterns.

Table 4. Payments summary for scenario 1

	January	February	March
Payments to Type 1			
January	$0	$36,000	$0
February	—	0	36,000
March	—	—	0
Total to Type 1	0	36,000	36,000
Payments to Type 2			
For January purchases	0	12,000	12,000
For February purchases	—	0	12,000
For March purchases	—	—	0
Total to Type 2	0	12,000	24,000
Total payments	$0	$48,000	$60,000

Table 5. Payments summary for scenario 2

	January	February	March
Payments to Type 1			
For January Purchases	$21,600	$14,400	$0
For February Purchases	—	21,600	14,400
For March Purchases	—	—	21,600
Total to Type 1	21,600	36,000	36,000
Payments to Type 2			
For January Purchases	0	24,000	0
For February Purchases	—	0	24,000
For March Purchases	—	—	0
Total to Type 2	0	24,000	24,000
Total payments	$21,600	$60,000	$60,000

Receipts versus Payments

In addition to payments to suppliers, the company has to pay for other parts of operations such as salaries, utilities, etc., which also need to be taken into account. These costs are relatively easy to estimate, especially since they do not require the compliance of outside forces (such as customers or suppliers). A cash budget or forecast can now be prepared. Table 6 shows a case budget or forecast based on these expense items for a three-month period.

Table 6. Summary of expenses

Item	Cost
Salaries	$12,000
Utilities	5,000
Finance costs	6,000
Marketing costs	2,300
Insurance	600
Vehicle expenses	3,000
Administrative expenses	4,000
Other running expenses	1,000
Total	**$33,900**

These expenses, along with payments to suppliers, make up the total amount to be paid. Assuming there are no other sources of cash besides those listed in tables 1, 2, and 3, all payments will have to be made from the cash receipts from sales. We can now prepare the complete cash forecasts (Tables 7 and 8).

Table 7. Cash budget for scenario 1

	January	February	March
Receipts (Table 1)	$150,000	$150,000	$150,000
Payments			
Suppliers (Table 3)	0	48,000	60,000
Running expenses (Table 6)	33,900	33,900	33,900
Total payments	**33,900**	**81,900**	**93,900**
Surplus cash	**$116,100**	**$68,100**	**$56,100**

Table 8. Cash budget for scenario 2

	January	February	March
Receipts (Table 3)	$49,500	$130,500	$145,500
Payments			
Suppliers (Table 5)	21,600	60,000	60,000
Running expenses (Table 6)	33,900	33,900	33,900
Total payments	**55,500**	**93,900**	**93,900**
Surplus or deficit	**—$6,000**	**$36,600**	**$51,600**

O. Othata

The two cash budgets as presented in Tables 7 and 8 clearly show the effect that receipt and payment patterns have on the cash available. In the scenario summarized in Table 7, whereby all sales brought in immediate cash, the company had a cash surplus at the end of each month. Table 8, on the other hand, predicts a deficit for January. For scenario 1 (Table 7) management's immediate task would be to answer the question "What to do with the surplus cash?" For scenario 2, management's task would be less enviable as the question would be "How and where to source the extra cash?"

Dealing with Deficits and Surpluses

As we have seen, a cash budget provides an indication of whether to expect a deficit or a surplus. Either outcome needs a plan of action from management. A surplus gives management a "good problem"—the task of looking for investment options or expenditure avenues. In contrast, dealing with a deficit is more difficult and stressful since success depends largely on other parties. Failure to adequately deal with a deficit can lead to collapse of a firm. In fact failure to deal with cash deficits is responsible for many African SME collapses. Let us consider the case of the deficit first.

Dealing with Deficit

The first step in dealing with a cash deficit is to understand why it has arisen. If the deficit is determined to have arisen because of a short-term dip in cyclical sales and/or a once-off expense, a common strategy is to negotiate a simple bank overdraft. Keep in mind that bankers are more likely to assist if they are approached before the shortage actually occurs and if the company is able to provide a clear indication of when the situation is likely to improve. If on the other hand, the deficit is due to problems with collections and is expected to last longer, then you may have to resort to one of these strategies:

- *Renegotiate terms with suppliers to delay payments*: This option is easiest with smaller suppliers, who may agree to being paid late. Developing good relationships with suppliers has been known to make even large suppliers agree to payment delays. Good negotiation skills are required to pull this option through.

- *Renegotiate terms with customers and offer early payment discounts to advance receipts*: Offering customers discounts for early or on-time payment is another simple, yet effective way to improve cash flow. The downside is that the amount received is lower than the actual invoice amount, so you should offer only modest discounts. Note that this method does not work well if the customers themselves are facing cash flow problems, which unfortunately is a likely scenario with African SMEs.

- *Factoring and discounting invoices:* Factoring invoices involves selling invoices to a third party (known as a "factor") at a discount. The factor then pays you the agreed amount for the invoice and in turn collects the full invoice amount from the debtor as per the original payment terms. The advantage of invoice factoring is that your company receives cash in advance, easing cash flow pressures. Invoice discounting is similar to factoring except that instead of selling invoices to a factor, the company borrows money from a third party using invoices as collateral for the loan. Both services are available to SMEs in most African countries.

- *Review monthly expenses to see if you can cut back on anything in order to decrease cash outflows:* This method involves having a look at expenses to see which may be avoided altogether and which may be paid later.

- *Enforce strict adherence to credit terms:* When possible, customers should be given reminders as the due dates of their invoices approach.

- *Engage professional debt collectors for bad debts:* In the case of customers that have defaulted on payments, it is best to hand their account over to professional debt collectors. But because this option comes at a cost, it is only substantial amounts that are worth handing over to debt collectors and even so, this should be a last resort.

- *Obtain short-term business loans:* Many African SMEs rely on short-term loans from financial institutions to solve short-term cash deficits. Some banks may even offer interest-free overdrafts.

Dealing with Surplus Cash

It is considered unwise in business to hoard large sums of cash. Conventional wisdom dictates that surplus cash should be invested so that more revenue is generated. The following are common investment avenues for SMEs, grouped according to the level of risk they entail.

- Low risk investment avenues
  - *Interest bearing bank deposits:* All banks offer deposit accounts which earn modest interest. The minor downside to such accounts is that many of them come with restrictions on accessing the money. Often the bank requires advance notice before you can withdraw funds.

- o *Corporate and government bonds*: Bonds are instruments issued by large corporations and governments which entitle the holder to receiving interest at specified intervals and ultimately the original amount when the bond expires. Because of the length of time involved (common bonds mature after 10 years), bonds should be considered only as a long-term investment option.

- High risk investment avenues
  - o *Buy shares in the stock market*: SMEs can buy shares in the stock market with the hope that the value of the shares will increase over time so that they can sell them at a profit at a later date. Further, SMEs can also receive dividends if the companies whose shares they have bought are profitable. The downside is that shares may lose value and companies may fail to declare dividends.

  - o *Acquire controlling interest in other firms*: This option involves investing in other firms through buying the majority of shares. The benefits of this option are that dividends received increase the cash flow, but this happens, of course, only if the acquired firm is profitable.

  - o *Diversify into other industries*: This approach involves investing in industries that are different from the one the SME is currently operating in.

  - o *Expand and improve operations*: Expanding and improving operations is largely regarded as the starting point for SME growth.

- Other avenues
  - o *Increase corporate social investment*: Corporate social investment involves helping communities achieve certain objectives through donations, sponsorships of events, and grants. Companies which engage in corporate social investment enhance their reputation, which in turn may attract more customers.

  - o *Offer more staff training*: Training of staff in various functional areas of the business (such as operations, marketing, finance, etc.) will likely help your company become more efficient and better achieve its goals. Unfortunately, in Africa SMEs spend relatively little on staff training, although SMEs that do provide training sometimes lament that once employees have received **further training, a large** percentage of them leave. There are ways to ensure this does not happen, and the possibility should not stand in the way of providing much-needed training for your staff.

o *Increase dividend and bonus payments:* Although strictly speaking paying dividends and bonuses is not an investment, receiving extra dividends can motivate shareholders to support the business when the need arise and paying bonuses can motivate staff to perform.

Summary

Although cash flow management is crucial, it remains a supporting act. Sound cash flow management without sound production, marketing, and general management is unlikely to bring any success. Cash has to be generated first before its flow can be managed. Similarly, sound marketing, production, and general management on their own can only lead a firm to generate revenues but not to collect the cash and put it to profitable use. Many profitable businesses that did everything else right are known to have collapsed because they failed to manage cash flows. So it is important that cash flow management be incorporated into the overall strategic plan and vision.

Sources

Ebben J., and A. Johnson (2011). Cash Conversion Cycle Management in Small Firms: Relationships with Liquidity, Invested Capital, and Firm Performance. *Journal of Small Business and Entrepreneurship* 24 (3): 381.

O. Othata

HUMAN RESOURCE MANAGEMENT IN AFRICAN AGRIBUSINESSES

Quinetta Roberson

Introduction

A company's human resources are the people that staff and operate it. Although individuals fulfill different roles in an organization, they are collectively responsible for production and service delivery, and ultimately organizational performance. As such, human resources can be distinguished from other material or financial resources (e.g., property, plant, equipment, cash, etc.). Consistent with this definition, human resource management refers to the practices and policies designed to govern employees and maximize their performance.

Research has highlighted the effects of human resource management on employee and organizational outcomes, suggesting, for example, that high-performance human resource practices increase employee satisfaction, commitment, and intent to remain with an organization (Kehoe and Wright 2013). By influencing employee behavior, research has also shown human resource practices to be associated with a number of financial benefits, including increased sales, profits, and stock value (Wright et al. 2005). Therefore, the management of people is a strategic function which contributes to organizational functioning and financial performance.

Because particular human resource practices tend to be complementary and mutually reinforcing, bundling practices together may help firms to achieve competitive advantage through people (Delery and Doty 1996). In particular, sets of practices collated around a firm's strategy or culture may focus employee behavior and drive business objectives. Other contextual factors, such as firm size or national culture, may be important considerations when organizing human resource practices into systems given their influence on the implementation of firm strategy.

Such human resource considerations apply not just to large businesses. Indeed, workforce alignment, the idea that, in a well-functioning company, the 'right' employees are doing the 'right' tasks at the 'right' time, is particularly applicable to small and medium enterprises (SMEs) (Collins, Ericksen, and Allen 2004). Workforce alignment can be achieved through appropriate selection, management, and motivation practices (Collins, Ericksen, and Allen 2004).

I have been a facilitator in the Making Markets Matter (MMM) program for 10 years. In my first year, I was eager to discuss human resource management best practices as they function in companies in North America and Europe and how they might be applied in an African business context. I quickly learned, however, that historical, political, economic, and cultural factors reduce the transferability of such practices, and thus their potential impact, to African SMEs. Therefore I began to use my experiences in the MMM program to open a dialogue on human resource management in Africa and discover those practices that have shown a consistently positive impact on employee and organizational performance.

This chapter shares my findings and discusses human resource management best practices in African SMEs. But before delving into the best practices, the chapter provides a general overview of human resource management as an organizational system with a review of specific practices for attracting, motivating, and retaining employees. As such, this overview is not specific to SMEs alone, but it is hoped that SME owners and managers will find it useful as a collection of potential management tools for their businesses. Next we will look at the role of context—specifically, the opportunities and challenges of being a small business and doing business in Africa—on the management of human resources. The chapter concludes with human resource best practices in agribusiness SMEs in Africa, as offered by participants in the MMM training program over the last 15 years.

Human Resource Management: A Conceptual Framework

Human resource management represents the personnel function in an organization. It encompasses practices and policies for planning, directing, and coordinating employee behavior. While the specific approaches used vary among firms, most human resource practices can be categorized into one of five major practice areas: staffing, performance management, training and development, compensation and rewards, and employee relations and retention (see Figure .1).

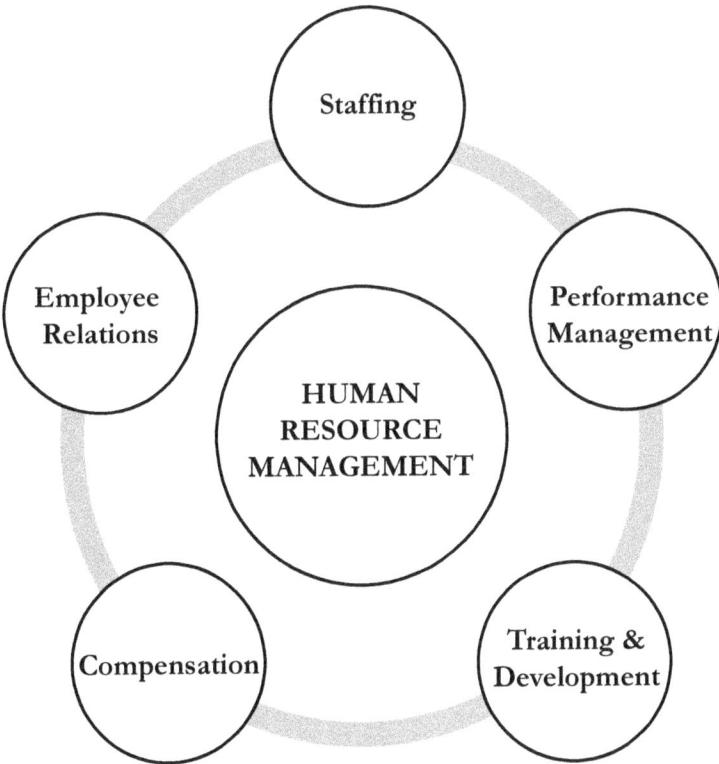

Figure 1. Components of human resource management

Staffing

Staffing is the process of acquiring employees consistent with the needs of an organization and getting them into the right positions. To have strategic impact, companies should first determine their current headcounts and what competencies are available in their current workforces. In addition, firms should do an environmental scan to forecast labor trends and future needs. Based on this information, they may recruit and select employees to fill positions and support business goals.

Recruitment is the process of generating a large pool of qualified candidates for a particular job. Organizations have a number of recruiting sources available to them, which may be distinguished in terms of internal and external sources. Internal sources are those that generate applicants from a firm's current workforce or use employees as a source of potential job candidates. For example, firms may use employee transfers and promotions, internal job postings, or employee referrals to create a pool of job candidates. External sources are those that seek candidates from outside the company, such as advertisements, employment agencies, or job fairs. To choose between sources, business leaders should consider cost, speed, ease of evaluation, and whether they have a need for candidates who have some experience with the organization.

Selection is the process of evaluating applicants for a particular job and deciding who best fits the position. Companies have a number of selection tools available to them, including applications and résumés, cognitive or other ability tests, work samples or job simulations, and references. They may also use interviews to determine how candidates will likely perform in a particular role. To choose the best selection tools, business leaders need to consider which ones are most useful for predicting future job performance. They should also consider using more cost-effective tools early in the selection process, when there is a larger pool of candidates, and saving comprehensive and/or expensive tools to decide between a shortlist of candidates in the latter stages.

Performance Management

Performance management is the process of evaluating employee performance and identifying areas of strength or improvement. It is a tool that can be used to determine employee training and development needs, and to motivate employee behavior that is consistent with a company's strategic goals. It can also be used to make administrative personnel decisions, such as pay, promotion, or terminations.

The primary tool used in performance management is the **appraisal**, which assesses how well employees are performing the activities that a job requires or demonstrating the competencies needed to do the job successfully. While performance appraisals can measure a variety of employee characteristics, formats that provide information on the demonstration of behaviors and/or achievement of results tend to be most valid and useful. For the most accurate evaluation, the person who has the most opportunity to observe employee performance, such as a manager or client, should complete the appraisal.

Feedback delivery is also a critical component of the performance management process. Managers should meet with each employee to review the appraisal ratings, identify strengths and weaknesses, and set goals for the next evaluation period. They should also determine how they can best support employees to help them achieve their and the organization's goals.

Training and Development

Training is the process of providing employees with learning opportunities to acquire new knowledge or skills or to address performance gaps. Companies should first conduct a needs assessment to identify performance requirements or training needs and determine instructional objectives, both of which may be used to design or select appropriate instructional programs. Training may be delivered in a variety of ways, including short courses, discussions, e-learning, simulations, or on the job. As a business leader, you should rely on cost-effective training methods that produce sustainable improvements in knowledge or skills and positively affect business performance.

Development is the process of providing employees with learning opportunities that go beyond the scope of their job descriptions and facilitate career progression. While many employee development programs are focused on cultivating future leaders, they may also prepare employees for other future job opportunities or impending organizational changes. Regardless of the objective, development is a dynamic and ongoing process that leverages employees' experiences to facilitate their growth and progress towards career goals.

Organizations may develop employees through various methods, including formal education programs, assessments, or job rotations. Employee development may also occur through **mentoring**, which provides career or psychological support via role modeling, or **coaching**, which provides feedback and reinforcement to help employees develop specific skills. While both mentoring and coaching are development tools based on one-to-one interactions, mentoring relationships tend to be between individuals with different levels of professional experience and of longer duration.

Compensation and Benefits

Compensation represents all of the rewards earned by employees in exchange for their work. There are three types of compensation: direct, or money received in the form of wages and salaries, and performance-based pay; indirect, or benefits and other rewards that are part of the employment contract between employer and employee; and nonfinancial, or recognition and other career-related opportunities. An organization must decide what pay mix, or allocation of the different types of compensation, it is going to use for employees.

Direct compensation may be given in the form of base or incentive pay. Base pay is a fixed amount of money that an employee receives on a regular basis in exchange for job performance. For example, employees will receive an hourly wage or annual salary for the performance of the tasks, duties, and responsibilities of their role. When determining base pay, business leaders must consider industry standards, where a job falls in an organization's hierarchy, and the job-relevant competencies that a candidate possesses. In addition to base pay, employees may receive incentive pay, or compensation that changes in amount based on their level of performance in a job, such as bonuses, stock options, or commissions.

Indirect compensation represents optional rewards provided to employees in addition to direct compensation received. Such rewards may come in a number of forms, including medical and health benefits, insurance, retirement benefits, vacation and other leave, and employee services (e.g., family, education, etc.). Organizations should decide which rewards to offer based on industry standards, how much flexibility to offer employees, and retention goals.

Nonfinancial compensation assists employees with balancing their work and life responsibilities and recognizes them for exemplary performance. Workplace flexibility benefits, such as flextime or telecommuting, allow employees to structure their job or workweek. Recognition benefits, such as praise from management or development opportunities, are cost-efficient yet motivate employee behavior. As a business leader, you should strive for a balance between your retention goals and the company's ability to complete core work in a quality and timely manner.

Employee Relations

Employee relations comprise the processes involved in maintaining employer–employee relationships and retention of employees in organizations. Many organizations administer employee relations via an employee handbook, which provides relevant information on employee rights and human resource policies, and ensures fair and consistent treatment. Others rely upon additional practices that facilitate a more proactive approach to managing employees and creating a high-performance culture.

A reactive approach to employee relations focuses on correcting poor performance and resolving employee grievances. Given that organizations typically expect employees to maintain standards of performance and conduct, disciplinary action processes are often established to correct substandard behavior or results. As employees typically expect organizations to maintain standards of fairness, organizations will also establish complaint procedures to maintain an impartial work environment.

A proactive approach to employee relations focuses on increasing your employees' level of engagement. Engagement is driven by how well employees understand their roles and responsibilities in the organization, how much enthusiasm they bring to their jobs, and how willing they are to invest discretionary effort to perform their jobs well. As a business leader you can drive engagement by company practices that increase employees' feelings of commitment to the job and organization, belongingness to the organization, and passion for their work.

Human Resource Management: The Role of Context

Research on human resource management provides guidance on practices to drive employee performance and organizational strategy. As interactions with numerous African SMEs through the MMM program show, however, features of the external environment in which African businesses operate may limit the generalizability or effectiveness of such practices. Specifically in African countries, certain economic, political, legal, and cultural factors may affect the suitability of human resource management practices that work in other parts of the world. Internal characteristics of small businesses may also reduce leaders' capacity for implementing traditional "best practices." Therefore it is important to consider how context can influence human resource management in African SMEs.

Economic indicators place most African countries among developing nations. For example, macroeconomic factors, such as gross domestic product and commodity prices, suggest a growing external demand for African goods and services. Trends in inflation and interest rates also establish Africa as an emerging market. Market fluctuation and uncertainties, however, highlight economic volatility. Thus, to sustain operations under such unstable growth, organizations operating in the African business context should take steps to manage and mitigate risk.

Worker mobility is also an important economic factor that may affect African businesses. While globalization has internationalized labor markets, with workers moving across geographic boundaries, the majority of employees in Africa derive from their country of origin. Unemployment rates and skill mixes are driven more by the availability of talent in local rather than national markets. Such migration trends are an important consideration for African businesses in forecasting labor demand vs. supply and staffing their workforces.

The political and legal climates of Africa present several operating challenges. The sociopolitical landscape is widely divergent, with some countries having no employment law in place, while others have regulations that are considered by some business leaders to be ambiguous or even restrictive. Similarly, past instances of discrimination and/or corruption within governments have given rise to labor unions, some of which have contentious relationships with businesses. Tribal, ethnic, and other divisions within the political landscape contribute to the challenges of leadership and business management. Thus, companies operating in Africa must be aware of, and comply with, established employment laws and regulations, but should also strive to maintain positive and transparent employer–employee relations.

Although languages, customs, and values differ throughout the continent, overarching cultural norms influence the way organizations do business in Africa. The culture is primarily one of a collective society, or one in which people see themselves as a member of a group or family ("we") rather than as an individual ("I"). As such, group solidarity and maintaining harmonious relationships are critical in business interactions. African culture may also be characterized in terms of high power distance, or an acceptance of hierarchical order based on power and status. With some exceptions (e.g., South Africa), less powerful people expect and accept the unequal distribution of power in an organization. The culture also has a longer-term orientation in the sense that there is a preference for maintaining traditions and historical norms. In such environments, leadership styles tend to be more authoritarian, although conflict resolution is done democratically or within a group environment. It is of course impossible to generalize for an entire diverse continent, but the take-home message is that whatever cultural nuances may characterize countries or regions in Africa, organizations should account for such influences in their day-to-day operations.

Internal firm characteristics of SMEs may also impact organizational functioning, including human resource management. Given their size, SMEs tend to operate with limited resources. Although there are resource constraints on all firms, the capacity of SMEs requires them to operate particularly efficiently and create economies of scope. Many small businesses are run and operated by an owner, who assumes responsibility for many of the firm's support functions (e.g., marketing, human resource management, etc.). Medium firms may rely on flat structures or hierarchies, which disperses responsibility for leadership and decision-making among a few people within an organization. Given the need to concentrate on core business activities yet with limited resources, organizations need formal human resource practices and policies to facilitate the efficient and effective management of employees. In addition, human resource systems should be designed to motivate maximum contribution and retention.

A defined organizational culture is vital for driving an organization's mission and directing employee behavior. By creating a shared set of beliefs and values, everyone in the workforce has a framework for how to set priorities, make decisions, and interact with others. Positive corporate cultures can also help organizations weather economic downturns and other market shifts, which may initiate organizational and/or workforce changes. While SMEs often have family-like cultures, creating and maintaining positive cultures of community and openness are particularly important to employee commitment and productivity, and subsequently organizational performance. Accordingly, human resource systems that support a firm's mission and value, treat employees equally, strengthen social ties, and facilitate open communication may be valuable to SMEs.

Human Resource Management in African SMEs: Lessons Learned

We have seen that a firm's human resources may serve as a source of competitive advantage and that certain practices are particularly useful in creating a positive workplace culture for all employees. But we have also observed that context—certain external and internal factors specific to African countries—may lessen the potential impact of human resource practices in African SMEs. Indeed this is what I observed in the Making

Markets Matter program, where some participants questioned the applicability of certain practices to their businesses. Listening to them I quickly realized that there was a need for human resource management models that recognize the uniqueness of the African and small business contexts. Therefore I started using the human resource management session in the MMM training program as a brainstorming session to explore human resource best practices in small agribusiness companies in Africa. From these discussions I have compiled best practices within each of the major human resource practice areas: staffing, performance management, training and development, compensation and rewards, and employee relations and retention.

Staffing

MMM participants highlighted the importance of having job descriptions for all positions in an organization. Job descriptions should specify the tasks, duties, and responsibilities of a position as well as the knowledge, skills, and abilities needed to perform well in that position. Job descriptions are critical to staffing processes as they provide managers with guidance on the desired qualifications for applicants and how to assess candidates for jobs.

While all business leaders would like to hire talent from top universities, participants noted that limited resources require them to use targeted sources to find employees that are highly motivated and likely to have a long career with the company. For example, one participant suggested rehiring former employees. Although organizations have to ensure that any behavior or performance problems have been corrected, former employees can be a valuable addition to a company given their training, experience, and familiarity with its corporate culture. Another participant suggested asking current employees to refer family members and friends to apply for open positions, as employees can likely assess who would be a good fit for the organization. Other stakeholders, such as customers or suppliers, might also be sources of potential applicants.

Because applicant pools may be small for African SMEs, available job candidates may not be qualified or a good fit for a position. Accordingly, participants highlighted the importance of considering potential candidates from the current workforce. They reasoned that while some training may be required to prepare a current employee for another position, the costs associated with training are likely to be less than those required to recruit and select someone from outside the organization. Because internal recruiting also strengthens morale, they recommended that all job vacancies be communicated throughout the organization and all employees be allowed to apply for any opening.

Given the importance of corporate culture to organizational functioning in African SMEs, participants emphasized the value of including cultural fit as a selection criterion. Specifically, after evaluating whether candidates have the competencies and capabilities to perform well in a job, hiring managers should evaluate the degree to which they share and demonstrate the organization's values. In addition to strengthening the culture, person–organization fit has been shown to increase employee commitment and citizenship and to decrease turnover.

Performance Management

MMM participants highlighted the importance of having formal and systematic processes of performance appraisal to motivate employee behavior and results. Given limited time resources, they suggested doing annual assessments of expected versus actual performance. Some participants described their approach to such assessments, which rely on the job description and rate employees on how well they complete the various duties and responsibilities of the job. Others described an approach that involves setting goals (or targets) and measuring employees' progress toward, or achievement of, those goals. While both methodologies may be effective, all participants noted the importance of having a fair way to compare employee performance throughout the organization and to make employment decisions (e.g., compensation, promotion, etc.). One participant also commented that empowering employees to monitor their own work and performance is useful for motivating employees and creating a performance culture.

Beyond the evaluation, participants discussed the importance of regularly providing employees with feedback on their performance. Giving employees information on how they are doing is useful for reinforcing appropriate behaviors and correcting performance deficiencies. In addition, discussing progress toward goals can help clarify expectations and motivate employee effort toward higher performance. Thus, participants thought that a best practice in the area of performance management was to hold regular (e.g., quarterly) sessions with individual employees to discuss goals, performance, strengths and weaknesses, and strategies for improvement. Some business owners also put in place forums for employees to discuss any problems that arise during the day—for example, a mobile phone dedicated for employee calls, or end-of-day meetings to discuss what worked well and what did not.

Training and Development

Given limited training and development budgets, MMM participants highlighted the importance of knowledge sharing within the company. For example, one business owner described the practice of sharing materials and key learning points from any workshop or seminar he attends with his staff. Another requires employees who attend external training programs to give a brief presentation of what they learned at monthly staff meetings. Another uses apprenticeships, or one-on-one training sessions between employees with a particular skill and those with less experience. There have also been discussions on the creation of a virtual "library" within the organization through which employees can share books, articles, and other learning resources.

Business owners also explained their need to be innovative about training opportunities given limited resources for sending employees to off-site training at a university or sponsored program. For example, one participant who has a sales company invites business partners to train employees on how to market their product. Another business owner has students train employees on how to use specific software programs and other technologies.

Many of the participants' best practices for developing employees focused on empowerment. Specifically, suggestions converged on giving different types of authority to different employees, but allowing them to make mistakes. Many participants recommended putting high-potential employees, or those with the ability and motivation to move up in the organization, in charge of daily operations to give them an opportunity to demonstrate their leadership potential. Some also mentioned allowing other employees to lead a team or project to allow them to practice certain leadership skills. Several business owners also use "stretch assignments," or activities that are beyond employees' current knowledge or skill level, to allow them to achieve and grow their capabilities.

Compensation and Benefits

MMM participants' best practices for compensation of employees primarily leverage indirect and nonfinancial forms of compensation and reward. Given rising health care costs for both employers and employees, they suggested providing access to social services. For example, one participant has the Department of Health bring a mobile clinic to the worksite monthly for health screenings. Similarly, another one subsidizes HIV/AIDS testing and treatment for employees. One business owner brings a social worker in periodically to discuss health and family issues with employees.

Participants also discussed other services to promote employee wellness and work–life balance. For example, several have created emergency funds from which employees can draw if they are experiencing a personal or family hardship. Some business owners compensate employees with food or transportation vouchers, depending on their particular needs. Others provide financial workshops, subsidized access to gyms, and additional indirect benefits.

In every MMM training program the importance of employee recognition was discussed. Participants highlighted a need to recognize both individual and team contributions to motivate and reward employees. They also noted that such recognition may be formal, such as awards or gifts, or informal—something as simple as a compliment when an employee does a good job.

Employee Relations

MMM participants knew the value of creating and maintaining a positive work climate and offered several best practices for facilitating cultures of trust and respect. For example, they suggested greeting employees by name every day, asking them about their families, and speaking with employees in their native dialects. They also suggested organizing social events with employees, such as lunches or end-of-the-year family gatherings, as team-building activities. Other strategies for developing a strong social environment were to offer volunteer opportunities that involve everyone in the company or invite employees to showcase their tribal or ethnic cultures.

To encourage knowledge-sharing, participants discussed their employee participation and communication practices. To involve employees in business planning and decision-making, many business owners created forums for them to share their ideas and perspectives. For example, one participant holds regular team meetings to get employees' thoughts and suggestions about new policies or practices. Another holds daily "office hours" for employees to come in to discuss any topic of interest. Several business owners also had strategies for circulating information to the workforce, including newsletters or e-mails to share updates on how the company is doing.

Conclusion

This chapter has focused on what is arguably the most important resource in a company—its people. I started by reviewing a set of human resource practices that are generally seen as best practices in North America and Europe. Working with African SMEs for the past 15 years has taught me, however, that one size does not fit all—those best practices are not necessarily suitable in the environment surrounding African businesses. But what is clear from the discussions with African SME owners and managers is that, while they may not employ traditional ("Western") best practices, African business leaders do in fact recognize the importance of human resource management and they do in fact have human resource management practices of their own. Their practices are innovative and resourceful, and they reflect the particular cultural and economic realities that surround African companies. They represent human resource management "on a shoestring"; while a company may not be in the position to offer many significant monetary rewards, owners and managers try to reward employees through social interactions that make them feel valued. And this point is key because it shows that, despite the challenges that surround their businesses, African business leaders recognize fully well that the basis of a company's success lies in a loyal, well-trained, and motivated workforce.

Sources

Arthur, J. B. (1994). Effects of Human Resource Systems on Manufacturing Performance and Turnover. *Academy of Management Journal* 37: 670–687.

Barney, J. (1991). Firm Resources and Sustained Competitive Advantage. *Journal of Management* 17: 99–120.

Barney, J. (1995). Looking Inside for Competitive Advantage. *Academy of Management Executive* 9(4): 49–61.

Collins, C., J. Ericksen, and M. Allen (2004). Human Resource Management Practices and Firm Performance in Small Businesses. Research Report on Phase 2 of Cornell University/Gevity Institute Study. Gevity Institute.

Delery, J. E., and D. H. Doty (1996). Modes of Theorizing in Strategic Human Resource Management: Tests of Universalistic, Contingency and Configurational Performance Predictions. *Academy of Management Journal* 39: 802–835.

Huselid, M. (1995). The Impact of Human Resource Management Practices on Turnover, Productivity, and Corporate Financial Performance. *Academy of Management Journal* 38: 635–672.

Kehoe, R. R., and P. M. Wright (2013). The Impact of High-Performance Human Resource Practices on Employees' Attitudes and Behaviors. *Journal of Management* 39(2): 366–391.

Wright, P. M., T. M. Gardner, L. M. Moynihan, and M. R. Allen (2005). The Relationship between HR Practices and Firm Performance: Examining Causal Order. *Personnel Psychology* 58: 409–446.

ADDING VALUE TO
AFRICAN INDIGENOUS FOODS:
THE CASE OF MORAMA BEANS

Jose Jackson

Introduction

The term "indigenous foods" typically refers to foods that grow in a particular area and cannot grow elsewhere; they are foods from the natural environment that have become part of the cultural food use patterns of a group of indigenous people. Examples of African indigenous foods include sorghum, phane caterpillars, lerotse, morama, baobab, and morula. Some, like morula, are well known and already commercialized globally. Others continue to remain on the margins and are sometimes referred to as underutilized, emerging, underexploited, wild, fringe, orphan, or traditional foods. Indigenous foods in Africa are valued and used by the communities where they are found, but often little, if any, documentation is available on their distribution, biology, and cultivation. They typically have weak or no formal supply systems and have received little attention from researchers, extension services, or policy and decision makers.

In recent years indigenous foods have received increasing attention for two reasons. One is the recognition that indigenous foods have unrealized potential for contributing to human welfare, in particular to generating incomes in low-income communities, food security, nutrition, and reduction of micronutrient deficiencies. Many indigenous foods have significant nutritional, culinary, medicinal, and other properties and are typically well adapted to specific agro-ecological niches and marginal land, and therefore would be suitable for scaled-up production in the areas where they are found. The second reason is that indigenous foods, at least some of them, represent new product alternatives for the growing African middle class, whose members have disposable incomes and place increasing emphasis on products that are health-conscious, environmentally friendly, and convenient to prepare. Clearly, these two reasons represent two rather different roles—and therefore marketing opportunities—for indigenous products, but the bottom line is that indigenous foods in Africa are yet to be widely commercialized, and therefore they present a potentially lucrative business opportunity for local agribusiness entrepreneurs.

Since its inception, the Making Markets Matter training program has worked with enterprises focused on product development from African indigenous foods. Participants have discussed the issues African small and medium enterprises (SMEs) should consider when developing new products from indigenous foods. The discussions have yielded some good ideas and different perspectives, some of which have been put into practice by the SMEs. To gather the learnings from this "collective experiment," this chapter looks at the processes involved in new food product development and uses the case of the indigenous morama bean to demonstrate some best practices SMEs can apply when developing new indigenous foods products.

Product Development Concepts

New product development (NPD) is a basic activity in the food industry. Every company has a product mix. For small companies it may be just one or two products, while large companies may have hundreds of products. Regardless of the number of products, the product mix is constantly evolving—old products are dying, some products are reaching maturity, others are contributing to rapid growth, and new products are being introduced. Achieving a dynamic product mix requires a far-sighted and organized product development program, one that is in line with the company's business strategy.

It is well known that African SMEs are central to the continent's food sector and are considered an engine of economic growth. During the past decade, NPD has increasingly been recognized as a critical factor in ensuring the continued survival of SMEs. Concurrently, the rate of market and technological changes has also accelerated, presenting a turbulent environment that requires new methods and techniques to successfully bring new products to the marketplace. At present, the typical African SME has limited technical know-how in product development; what drives innovation, however, is networking with customers, suppliers, and other food companies as well as travel to new locations in search of product ideas. But NPD is likely to attain more importance in the SME sector in the coming years; companies will need to innovate to survive.

Successful product development programs encompass everything from product improvement and product line extension to product relaunch and product innovation. Importantly, all levels of the organization should be involved, from top management to the machine operator on the line; in short, product development needs to be integrated across the company and requires strong leadership from top management. These ideas are not new; in fact, in the early 1960s it was recognized that product development begins with management looking at business strategy, then working through the product strategy to the new product area definition (Earle and Earle, 2008). With time, as knowledge of business strategy improved, NPD grew to include new elements such as postlaunch evaluation, product concept development, integration of the consumer into product design and testing, and integration of market and technical research.

NPD is a major part of any manufacturing process because products have a limited lifespan, and new products need to be developed to replace phased-out ones and keep the company in business. Just as the product life cycle has various stages, NPD can be broken down into discrete phases as indicated in Table 1. These include idea generation, screening, development and testing, business analysis, market testing, technical implementation, commercialization, and new product pricing.

The NPD process may seem hard to attain for often cash-strapped SMEs. Yet, SMEs need to think about how they can adapt the product development process to their realities, because without it, new food products are more likely to fail than to succeed. Failure rates as high as 90% to 95% have been observed, and SMEs simply cannot afford to go through too many fruitless cycles of product development before they go out of business. Given such

Table 1: The New Product Development Process (Brands and Kleinman, 2010).

Phase	Detailed tasks
Idea generation	Ideas for new products can be obtained from basic research using a SWOT analysis, market and consumer trends, company's R&D department, competitors, focus groups, employees, salespeople, trade shows.
Idea screening	The object is to eliminate unsound concepts prior to devoting resources to them through questions such as will the customer in the target market benefit, size and growth forecasts of target market, current or expected competition, industry sales and market trends, technical feasibility to manufacture, and profitability when manufactured and delivered
Idea testing	Develop marketing and engineering details, investigate Intellectual Property issues and patent databases, identify target market and decision maker in the purchasing process, select key product features to be incorporated, identify benefits that the product will provide and evaluate how consumers will react to the product.
Business analysis	Estimate the likely selling price based upon competition and customer feedback, sales volume based upon size of market, and profitability and break-even point.
Market testing	Produce physical prototype or mock-up, test product (and its packaging) in typical usage situations, conduct focus group customer interviews or introduce at trade show, make adjustments if necessary, and produce an initial run of the product and sell it in a test market area to determine customer acceptance.
Technical implementation	Initiate new program, finalize quality management system, estimate resources, publish requirements and tech communications , plan engineering operations and supplier collaboration, publish logistics plan and resource plan, program review and monitoring, plan for contingencies ("what-if" planning).
Commercialization	Launch product, produce and place advertisements and other promotions, fill distribution pipeline with product, and conduct critical path analysis.
Product pricing	Impact of new product on the entire portfolio, value analysis (internal and external), competition and alternative technologies, differing value segments (price, value, and need), product costs (fixed and variable), forecast of unit volumes, revenue, and profit

J. Jackson

volatile market conditions, a key recommendation for SMEs is that they should integrate the marketing function into food NPD. In other words, marketing should be central to the thinking about new products, not just an afterthought. Of course we cannot expect that all African SMEs will employ cutting-edge NPD processes overnight, but some enterprises, in particular those in competitive industries like food processing, have begun to engage in more advanced NPD processes, a trend that is likely to continue. Key issues for SMEs to consider when they contemplate entering the indigenous food market are the necessity of having a clear understanding of the value chain, the specific product to target, and the competitors already out there.

Morama Bean Case Study

Let us now turn to the case study of the morama bean (*Tylosema esculentum*) to illustrate the process of new product development for an African indigenous food. The case of morama has been presented and discussed in Making Markets Matter, and, while the product itself is not on the market, product development and market testing are already underway. To make the NPD process easy to follow, the sections below refer back to Table 1.

Morama is indigenous to Southern Africa, so our example focuses specifically on developing new morama products for the countries in which the legume can be found (Botswana, Namibia, and South Africa). When selecting an indigenous food for product development, it is important to ask the following questions:

- Is the indigenous food currently used by the local population as either food or feed?

- Does the indigenous food have a high quality?

- Can we develop a wide variety of potential formulations from the indigenous food?

- Is there sufficient supply available for processing operations?

- Will consumers find the products acceptable

- Are there sufficient numbers of consumers who might buy the product?

These questions illustrate that developing a new product from an indigenous food requires careful consideration. Most importantly, the question ties together food science and marketing considerations, as recommended above. Before we go further into outlining how the NPD process may unfold, let us first learn about the raw material—the morama bean itself.

What is the Morama Bean?

The morama bean is an underutilized oilseed native to arid and semi-arid regions of Botswana, Namibia, and South Africa and forms part of the diet of indigenous populations. Morama beans are sometimes eaten when they are still immature green beans, but most of them are consumed as mature beans, when the seeds are surrounded by hard woody seed coats reddish to brownish in color (Figure 2). The wild growing morama bean has remained underutilized largely because it has not been domesticated, although indigenous communities use it as a source of food, feed, shelter, and medicine. The morama bean has highly favorable nutritional properties and contains components that may contribute to alleviating certain diseases. It therefore has enormous potential value, which needs to be exploited for the further benefit of the communities. This indigenous leguminous oilseed offers African SMEs a food resource that could improve the livelihoods of the communities in which it is found growing.

Figure 2. Green (1) and mature (2) morama bean (*Tylsoema esculentum*) (Photos: W. Chingwaru)

Perhaps the most important characteristic and value-added potential of the morama bean is its high nutritional quality, and it is this feature that SMEs should exploit to capture the market. Its fat content ranges between 24% and 48%, which is comparable to commercial vegetable oils such as sunflower seed and rapeseed and twice that of soybeans. Moreover, the fat is "good" fat—the type promoted by the food industry as "heart healthy" and which is also found in olive oil. Morama can therefore be a potential substitute for olive oil.

The protein content of morama ranges from 29% to 39%, a higher proportion than in most other beans. Most importantly it contains all the essential amino acids. The high protein content of morama beans offers great potential for improving the nutritional composition of staple cereals that have low protein contents.

Morama is also a good source of micronutrients (minerals and vitamins) such as calcium, iron, magnesium, phosphate, potassium, zinc, B vitamins (thiamine, riboflavin, nicotinic acid), vitamin C, and vitamin E. In small amounts these are critical for the healthy functioning of the body and some have been shown to be anticarcinogenic (may ward off cancer) and anti-inflammatory. The mineral and vitamin composition is important since large percentages of the population in Africa are deficient or at risk of inadequate intake of micronutrients.

The carbohydrate content of morama beans ranges from 19% to 24%. The plant contains a large amount of insoluble dietary fiber, more than peanuts and soybeans. Sufficient intake of insoluble fiber is associated with a reduction in diabetes, cholesterol, and colon cancer risk factors.

In short, morama is a healthy plant with great potential benefits. The next step is deciding which products might best harness the positive qualities.

The Product: Morama Milk

With morama bean having so many positive qualities, you, as the entrepreneur, may be tempted to make a number of products from it. Table 1 lists a variety of value-added product possibilities. As you narrow down your options, you will want to carefully consider each of these, for each product trying to answer the questions listed above about the manufacturing process, the existing market environment including consumer demand, competition, distribution channels, pricing, and promotional strategies. Of the products listed in Table 1, many—or perhaps all—have the potential to be successful products; let us choose one, morama milk, to see how the NPD process might unfold.

Morama milk is a creamy white water extract of morama beans that closely resembles dairy milk or soy milk in appearance and composition. It can be consumed as a refreshing and nutritious beverage similarly to dairy milk or soy milk, or it can be used as nutritional supplement in infant food providing additional protein, energy, and other nutrients to vulnerable populations if the supply of dairy milk is inadequate. It can also be used as a dairy milk alternative, which is an important attribute given the increasing numbers of lactose-intolerant consumers globally. Research on the quality of morama milk indicates that it is has high levels of protein, fat, minerals, and vitamins and compares favorably with cow milk and soy milk. Morama milk has been shown to have a shelf-life of up to seven days, which is similar to cow milk.

Table 1. Potential processing opportunities for the morama bean

Food	Processing	Uses
Morama milk	Milling, grinding, filtration, pasteurization, homogenization, packaging	Beverage
Morama oil	Solvent extracted/mechanically pressed of whole morama beans	Cooking oil, salads, cosmetic oil
Morama butter	Milling and grinding of whole morama beans to a paste	Confectionery
Morama flour	Milling of morama beans to fine particles; may include defatting first to produce a high protein flour	Supplement to staple cereal flours
Morama texturized foods	Milled flour extruded into various shapes	Snacks, breakfast cereals, meat analogues
Morama nuts	Whole morama dry roasted	Roasted nuts whole or chopped
Morama biscuits, cookies, muffins, bread, cake	Morama and wheat flours and other ingredients baked into snack foods	Baked snack foods
Morama roast	Morama flour and other spices baked as a meat-like loaf	Meat analogue
Morama ice cream	Morama powder added to mix for ice cream	Frozen snack food
Canned morama beans in tomato sauce	Whole morama beans thermally processed in a sauce	Savory cooked beans

Source: Jackson et al. 2010

Having made morama milk, we have established that we have a good quality product that appears to have similar—or even superior—characteristics as other similar products on the market today. But today's marketplace for foods is crowded, so before we can go into production, it is important to assess carefully the existing market and competing products, and then use the information gathered to determine exactly where to market and sell our product and what marketing messages to use. Let us turn to these questions now.

The Competition: Who Is in the Market Now?

To decide whether there is a place for morama milk in the market, we must first carefully measure morama milk against existing products with which it will compete in local, regional, and international markets. The market for nondairy milk drinks is on the increase due to growing levels of milk intolerance and allergies. Another nondairy alternative, soy milk, is available in nearly every supermarket in South Africa and to a lesser extent in Namibia and Botswana. Many supermarkets also carry rice or oat milk. These products vary in quality and especially taste. At present the main obstacle in the way of soya drinks becoming a staple food is the fact that they are lesser known than dairy milk. They also cost more, because in many countries dairy farmers receive subsidies, which result in lower milk prices. Finding a product to compete with cow milk in terms of price, quality, and taste is a tall order, yet one for which there is a market.

Clearly, one major competitor will be soy products. Soy products are also highly nutritious, soy is grown commercially, and there has been an aggressive marketing campaign for its use, especially within Africa. Soy milk alone is estimated to generate roughly US$1 billion in sales annually; it therefore already has a significant market share of the nondairy milk drinks. Soy product development is the result of increased consumer demand owing to increased society-wide consciousness of health issues. For example, soy milk is believed to lower cholesterol and prevent cancer, and consumers are able to drink it without the adverse effects associated with lactose breakdown.

Can Morama Milk Compete?

There is no doubt that the competition is strong, and morama milk producers would have to convince people to change their long-standing habit of drinking dairy or soy milk to drinking milk made from a wild plant. Key questions that they will need answers to are: What percentage of Botswana households currently drink soy milk? What is soy milk's share of the total milk category in Botswana? What motivates consumers to purchase soy milk and can this be applied to morama milk? Furthermore, why do some people associate soy with poor taste even if they have never tasted it? And is this likely also the case with morama milk?

What Is the Potential Target Market?

At least initially, it would make sense to market morama products in Botswana, Namibia, and South Africa, where the beans grow in the wild. The three countries are home to about 50 million people of diverse social and cultural backgrounds with a large number of ethnic groups, religions, and languages. With growing disposable incomes, urbanization, increasingly formalized markets, and growing consumer awareness in terms of health, sustainability, and social responsibility issues in these countries, the market for niche or specialty products has been growing and presents opportunities for new and innovative products. This creates opportunities for the commercialization of new products based on morama.

The retail environment in Botswana, Namibia, and South Africa is dominated by a number of large groups, which account for a significant proportion of retail sales. Five major retailers account for 86% of the market in South Africa, 80% in Botswana, and 73% in Namibia. The figures suggest a high level of retail concentration in all three of these countries, which means that the retail environment may be suitable for niche morama products, that is, morama products marketed as a specialty product catering to a certain segment of the market (e.g., health conscious consumers).

Pricing

Since morama milk will compete with well-established products and brands that are already commercialized, it may well prove difficult for it to compete on price alone. Rather morama milk will need to do so based on its health benefits or other novel value identified. Without such claims it may prove challenging to compete with the established products.

With regard to consumer preferences, we have gleaned some information from a brief survey conducted in the target markets with potential consumers, in which we asked whether they were buying competing products already, and, were morama milk available for purchase, how much they would be willing to pay for it. Information on the purchasing characteristics of consumers who already buy competing products in the three countries indicates that they are aware of competitors to morama milk and buy them on an almost monthly basis, spending on average US$4 to US$16 monthly. In terms of product benefits, these same consumers appear to be aware of the nutritional value of morama, although awareness was greater among consumers in South Africa and Namibia than in Botswana. None of the consumers interviewed had knowledge about the phytochemical or disease-preventing properties of morama; perhaps it is these features that may best be highlighted to give the product an edge over competitors in the market. Morama milk needs to have at least similar product performance to competing products.

The consumer survey also included questions about pricing. The feedback from consumers indicates that they are interested in a product like morama as long as it is priced the same as or lower than competing products. The reason for this is that consumers are reluctant to pay higher prices for unknown products. A small subset of consumers are willing to support indigenous or natural value-added products even if they are a bit more expensive than competing nonindigenous products. In short, consumer preferences suggest that the best marketing strategy for morama milk may be to match the price of the competition to the extent possible and at the same time play up the unique features of the product such as its health properties and the fact that it is a local product that contributes to the livelihood of low-income communities.

What Marketing Messages Should We Use?

The commercialization of morama milk would be impeded by marketing messages that fail to offer significant benefits and products that are relatively expensive. Consumer research also showed, however, that in the case of long-life milk products purchasing choices are primarily driven by the health benefits of the product rather than price. This pattern is usually indicative of products considered a luxury by consumers, and for such purchases the focus is on product attributes rather than price.

Conclusion and Lessons Learned

Based on the above analysis of the morama market and the potential consumers, a number of strategies for commercializing morama milk in Botswana, Namibia, and South Africa are possible. Let us summarize our findings. First, morama milk needs to have at least similar product performance as competing products in terms of consumer acceptability. Second, the differentiating health benefits of morama milk need to be clearly conveyed to consumers. This is especially important since most consumers are currently not even aware of the benefits of consuming soy and some, particularly in South Africa, were unfamiliar with morama. Third, we have learned that consumers are acutely aware of the balance between value and price of products; therefore, morama products will need to reflect perceived value. Since potential consumers of morama products appear to be price sensitive, morama products would likely need to be priced at or lower than the price of competing products in order to convince consumers to give morama milk a try.

In terms of a marketing strategy for morama milk, the product could be placed in the market as a nondairy milk supplement with health benefits similar to soy milk, in various formal and informal retail networks in the target countries. The marketing messages for morama milk should focus on the unique benefits and characteristics of the product. As we have learned, indigenous foods like morama beans have important nutritional qualities and contain many phytochemicals with potentially health-promoting properties, and as such can be marketed in high-value niche markets.

It is also important to remember that morama milk is just one commercial application of the raw material, there are several other possible applications (products) and the key is to screen and select options that are important and acceptable to consumers. Further, morama bean is clearly just one example of the many underutilized indigenous species with great agricultural potential, one that can provide a unique strategic opportunity to address and support food security efforts and improve the livelihoods of vulnerable populations. What is good about morama is that in addition to developing whole foods, product development can also be tailored toward developing morama ingredients with novel functional properties.

A considerable focus of this chapter was to demonstrate the potential of marketing morama and specifically morama milk. What has been shown to work with other indigenous products is to commercialize using a partnership model with businesses that already have commercial interests in similar products to the prototype morama products. For example, African SMEs interested in morama milk processing could link up with a dairy milk or soy milk processor to commercialize morama milk. Such a partnership could involve existing business enterprises as well as the rural communities where the raw material is collected.

As with many things, there are oftentimes rules that can contribute to success, and in new product development this is certainly the case. Below we list the seven rules in product development as identified by Leatherhead Food Research (2014) that are particularly applicable to NPD in SMEs.

Rule 1: Always taste your own products, neat as well as with the host food. Tasting sessions are an integral part of product development and you should taste and re-taste repeatedly. Taste yourself, get col-leagues to taste, and of course conduct consumer tastings. When developing food products, it is easy to just have a quick taste straight out of the bottle or jar, and this kind of tasting is needed. But it is also important to taste your product in the way it is expected to be consumed. For example, taste morama milk alone, but also as it is to be used in cereals or with coffee.

Rule 2: Let the products do the talking. After spending months developing and perfecting your new product comes the most difficult task of all—convincing your senior management colleagues to proceed to launch. And even after sorting out the supply chain and hitting the right margin, there is always the chance that someone will taste the product and dislike it. Have faith in your product and do not be afraid to use it to make your point.

Rule 3: Get close to marketing. The relationship with the marketing function is the most important one for a product developer. Regular contact and tasting sessions are vital, including discussions on the marketing messages and on-pack information that is being developed.

Rule 4: Use scientific data. There is need to analyze the products thoroughly in order to set specifications and define quality control procedures; careful use of selected data can be important in many ways. For example, in order to include health claims about morama milk in the marketing messaging, there is need for data to support the specific claim.

Rule 5: Consider the factory and supply chain. The start of any product development exercise is likely to be in the kitchen or development laboratory, and at this point the factory can seem a long way away. It is important, however, to at least think about the likely factory unit operations that may eventually apply and to design some robustness into your products at an early stage. The supply chain from the factory to the supermarket shelf will also influence the product quality. If this is of concern, simulations during product development should be incorporated.

Rule 6: Be an ambassador for your product. NPD takes a long time, perhaps weeks in the kitchen, laboratory, pilot plant, and factory developing the product. Nobody will be more committed than you to the success of your product. Check the local supermarkets soon after launch and investigate any issues. You must protect your product against attempts to ruin the quality through cost-savings.

Rule 7: Be careful with ingredients. It is convenient when developing a product to purchase a new ingredient at the local supermarket. This is fine during the early stages, when you are coming up with the chef's quality benchmark, but you will quickly need to revert to the industrial ingredients that will eventually be used in production. At an early stage of the project consider the markets in which your product will be sold to be sure that the ingredients you use are allowed in all of the markets.

As we can see, the first is concerned with tasting the products; rules 2 and 3 are concerned with how to communicate effectively with colleagues in other functions, especially marketing; and rules 4 to 7 are concerned with external factors that can affect the success of the product in the marketplace. In SMEs there may well be a single person filling the role of general manager, marketing manager, and consumer research manager, so you may be responsible for implementing all of the rules. The key thing to know is that the entire new product development process is an ever-evolving testing platform where errors will be made, designs will get trashed, and losses may be incurred. Having your entire team work in tight synchronicity will ensure the successful launch of goods or services, even if reinventing your own wheel. Productivity during product development can be achieved if, and only if, goals are clearly defined along the way and each process has contingencies clearly outlined on paper.

Sources

Amarteifio, J., and D. Moholo (1998). The chemical composition of four legumes consumed in Botswana. *J. Food Compos. Anal.* 11: 329–332.

AT Kearney (2014). *The 2014 African Retail Development Index: Seizing Africa's Retail Opportunities.* AT Kearney.

Bower, N., K. Hertel, J. Oh, and R. Storey (1988). Nutritional Evaluation of Marama Bean (*Tylosema esculentum*, Fabaceae): Analysis of the Seed. *Economic Botany* 42: 533–540.

Brands, R. F., and M. J. Kleinman (2010). *Robert's Rules of Innovation: A 10-Step Program for Corporate Survival.* New Jersey: John Wiley.

Brigelius-Flohé, R. (2006). Bioactivity of Vitamin E. *Nutr. Res. Rev.* 19: 174–186.

Earle, M. D., and R. L. Earle (2008). Creating New Foods. The Product Developer's Guide—The **Web Edition.** http://www.nzifst.org.nz/creatingnewfoods/ (accessed February 3, 2015).

Hoban, T. J. (1998). Improving the Success of New Product Development. *Food Technology* 52(1): 46–49.

Hollingsworth, P. (1996). Developing Food for the Next Millennium. *Food Technology* 50(6): 110–118.

Hollingsworth, P. (1998). New Rules for Success in Food Research. *Food Technology* 52(5): 76–79, 216.

Holse, M., S. Husted, and Å. Hansen (2010). Chemical Composition of Marama Bean (*Tylosema esculentum*): A Wild African Bean with Unexploited Potential. *J. Food Comp. Anal.* 23(6): 648–657.

Jackson, J. C., K. G. Duodu, M. Holse, M. D. Lima de Faria, D. Jordaan, W. Chingwaru, A. Hansen, A. Cencic, M. Kandawa-Schultz, S. M. Mpotokwane, P. Chimwamurombe, H. L. de Kock, and A. Minnaar (2010). The Morama Bean (*Tylosema esculentum*): A Potential Crop for Southern Africa. *Advances in Food and Nutrition Research* 61: 187–246.

Jaenicke, H., and I. Hoeschle-Zeledon (eds.) (2006). *Strategic Framework for Underutilized Plant Species Research and Development, with Special Reference to Asia and the Pacific, and to Sub-Saharan Africa.* Colombo, Sri Lanka: International Centre for Underutilised Crops; and Rome, Italy: Global Facilitation Unit for Underutilized Species. http://www.underutilized-species.org /documents/publications.

Jeffery, M. (1998). Beating the Odds in New Product Development. *The World of Ingredients* (January/February): 20–24.

KPMG (2014). *Fast-Moving Consumer Goods in Africa Sector Report.* South Africa: KPMG Africa.

Leatherhead Food Research. (2014) Top 10 rules for product development. http://www.leatherheadfood.com/top-10-rules-for-product-development (accessed on March 27, 2015)

Mabaya, E., and D. Jordaan (2010). Morama Bean Value Chain Analysis. Annual Report Marama II Project, Copenhagen, Denmark.

Maruatona, G. N., K. G. Duodu, and A. Minnaar (2010). Physicochemical, Nutritional and Functional Properties of Marama Bean Flour. *Food Chem.* 121: 400–405.

Matthews, R. (1997). Efficient New Product Introduction: Shattering the Myths. *Progressive Grocer* (July Supplement): 8–12.

Mitei, Y. C., J. C. Ngila, S. O. Yeboah, L. Wessjohann, and J. Schmidt (2008). NMR, GC-MS and ESI-FTICR-MS Profiling of Fatty Acids and Triacylglycerols in Some Botswana Seed Oils. *J. Am. Oil Chem. Soc.* 85: 1021–1032.

Mpotokwane, S. M. and K. P. Walker (2012). A Survey of Botswana's Indigenous Foods and Their Processing Technologies. Project report. Kanye, Botswana: National Food Technology Research Centre.

Serrano, J., and I. Goni (2004). Role of Black Bean *Phaseolus vulgaris* on the Nutritional Status of Guatemalan Population. *Arch. Latinoam. Nutr.* 54: 36–44.

Sloan, A. E. (1998). Food Industry Forecast: Consumer Trends to 2020 and Beyond. *Food Technology* 52(1): 37–44.

Surak, J. (1996). New Food Product Development. *The World of Ingredients* (March/April): 31–35.

Tyler, L. (1998). Asia Beyond 2000: Reviewing Trends in Tastes and Eating Habits. *The World of Ingredients* (March/April): 48–54.

UNICEF (2004). *Micronutrient Initiative; Vitamin and Mineral Deficiency, A Global Progress Report.* UNICEF.

U.S. Department of Agriculture (2007). National Nutrient Database for Standard Reference, Release 21. http://www.ars.usda.gov/nutrientdata (accessed May 12, 2012).

Will, M. (2008). *Promoting Value Chains of Neglected and Underutilized Species for Pro-Poor Growth and Biodiversity Conservation. Guidelines and Good Practices.* Rome, Italy: Global Facilitation Unit for Underutilized Species.

Young, J. (1998). New Product Development: Winner and Losers—A Personal Perspective. *The World of Ingredients* (July/August): 12–14.

STRATEGIC COMMUNICATION FOR AFRICAN AGRIBUSINESS SMES

Ndunge Kiiti

Introduction

Globally, small and medium enterprises (SMEs) are applauded for their tremendous contribution to economic growth (Ozigbo and Ezeaku 2009). They are often described as the 'engine' of growing economies demonstrated by their ability to innovate (Akomea-Bonsu and Sampong 2012), create jobs and wealth, use local or indigenous resources, facilitate industrialization, and promote rural and urban development (Ariyo 2005). But SMEs also face many challenges such as lack of internal capabilities, access to capital, and local infrastructure (Akomea-Bonsu and Sampong 2012). Increasingly, unpredictable and changing environments require leaders, across all industries, to manage change more effectively. For SMEs, a key to productive change management is the ability to communicate to stakeholders and to develop regular sources of feedback to ensure messages are diffused throughout the organization as necessary (Eisenberg, Johnson, and Pieterson 2015). But do most SMEs in Africa have a strategic communication plan? If they do not, what are the barriers to developing one? If they do, is there a forum or way that best practices can be shared so others can learn and adopt the relevant and appropriate methodologies for their business? What policies can facilitate a more effective use of communication by SMEs?

These are all questions that will be addressed in this chapter as numerous studies have shown that strategic communication can strengthen the ability of SMEs to compete more effectively at multiple levels—locally, nationally, regionally, and globally.

Why Strategic Communication?

Definition and Conceptual Framework

What do we mean when we talk about communication? While the definition of communication can vary, ultimately communication assumes there is some transfer of information or knowledge in an effort to create shared meaning. Traditional communication concepts and theories often assume communication has to be one-way, from the *sender*, who often controls the message, to the *receiver*, who becomes the decoder or 'interpreter.' It is based on the *trickle-down* approach, which allows those in control of the process to ignore or marginalize those with limited access or power. But how this information is shared, transferred, or used determines the effectiveness and earnestness of the process. Most contemporary communication scholars argue that feedback within a dialogical and participatory process is central to effective communication, whether verbal or nonverbal. Communication is transactional—something that sender and receiver do together as they work to understand each other (White 1999; Mody 2003). This concept of interaction is key to the functioning of any business or organization.

Strategic communication is the intersection of management strategy and communication. It is the use of communication in an effective way to help align a company or organization's strategy or overall positioning to ensure the mission is achieved. It involves making informed communication choices in order to achieve a desired outcome (Argenti, Howell, and Beck 2005; Hallahan et al. 2007; Thomas and Stephens 2015). From a management perspective, Jarzabkowski, Balogun and Seidl have emphasized the importance of the strategic components describing these practices as "actions, interactions, and negotiations of multiple actors and the situated practices that they draw upon in accomplishing that activity" (2007, 8). This can be achieved by drawing upon various methods of communication. Figure 1 illustrates a selected list of various types of communication used by most organizations, including SMEs.

N. Kiiti

Table1. Selected types of communication media

Interpersonal Communication	Social Media	Traditional Media
Personal and relational oriented	Focus is digital and interactive	Mainly mass media or broadly distributed
• Face-to-face (verbal or nonverbal) • Discussion groups or forums • Extension visits • Cellular phones (controversial)	• Twitter • Facebook • YouTube • Instagram • Wikis • E-mail • Websites • Cellular phones (platform for transactions)	• Newspapers • Television • Radio • Books • Magazines • Film, video • Brochures • Photography

Globally, as the field of communication has grown exponentially, there has frequently been an overlap in the types of communication and the formats or channels used for message delivery. For instance, most of the traditional media (e.g., newspapers, books, television, radio, newsletters, etc.) could all be made available in digital format on the Internet. This redefines and broadens access to information. So for any SME, a manager or leader must ensure that the organization's competences are developed to effectively use a broad array of communication methods to reach the targeted audiences at all levels.

Effective Strategy: The Communication–Management Link

Fann and Stephens (2015) carried out an extensive literature review to explore the link between management strategy and communication. They established three themes that are critical for businesses, big and small: understanding the role of stakeholders, aligning the organization's strategic position, and communicating at multiple levels.

In any business or organization, there are many stakeholders. The key is to identify who they are, what their role in or linkage to the organization is, and how to engage them effectively for positive outcomes. For SMEs, this means defining how stakeholders, whether internal (e.g., employees) or external (e.g., customers), can shape the organization's strategy and mission. This is emphasized by John Baker (2008) when he argues, "Leaders fail because no matter how outstanding the strategic thinking, which is typically generated at the top of the organization, it is only as good as it is understood and executed at every level in the organization." This, for example, is a good reminder that internal stakeholders, like employees, can inform and shape a business's mission and strategy. Often employees are part of social networks that companies target with marketing messages. If facilitated effectively, employees can help amplify these messages using their own channels of communication. 'Strategic' does not necessarily mean or equate 'to control' and 'power by top management,' as is often perceived.

Thus, for most SMEs, strategic alignment to achieve a mission may mean different approaches and various levels of achieving it. As seen in the example above, aligning internally with employees or externally with the industry landscape is an important step because this alignment defines the most strategic communication for the specified audience. Again, SMEs must continually recognize that audiences, whether internal or external, require targeted messages communicated through appropriate channels or methods.

The task of understanding how communication can operate by crossing many boundaries at multiple levels is complex. It is about conceptualizing or building a system. What works best for one SME may not work for another. Building bridges and linkages among stakeholders at different levels helps establish an ongoing process of strategic communication that links individuals to the organization's desired outcomes. Figure 2 illustrates the linkages between communication and management, especially as pertains to marketing. The space where business management, marketing, and communication overlap is where SMEs must build their strategic communication approach.

Because of the complexities of ensuring that strategic communication is effective within a business context, SMEs must draw on this type of integrated approach or framework, which is stakeholder-centric and data driven (Niemann 2005).

Understanding Communication as a System

If people are the driving engine behind organizations, then communication or interaction is the fuel that keeps them moving—whether forward or backward. Organizations cannot function without communication. Many practitioners have suggested that effective communication is the foundation of successful organizations or SMEs. For an SME to have a viable and effective life span it must develop a well-structured communication system (Magagula 2008).

Figure 1. Strategic integrated communication in relation to management (Source: Adapted from Niemann 2005, 106).

What are the building blocks of this communication system? It is important for an SME to understand the process and the resources or assets at their disposal (or lack thereof) as part of building a sound communication system based on the conceptual model outlined in Figure 2.

The Process

The process of building a communication system entails many essential aspects, but this section will focus on the communication audit as a strategy plan appropriate to organizational culture. A communication audit is an assessment that helps a business or organization to identify the strengths and weaknesses of past and current internal and external communications. The communication strategy aims to strengthen the relevant aspects of current approaches while developing untapped opportunities for future communications relevant to one's business. In essence, it is carrying out a SWOT (Strengths, Weaknesses, Opportunities, Threats) analysis focused on the communication aspects of the business.

To effectively carry out a communication audit that can be used to build a future strategy, Cornelissen (2004) posits that a business or organization must consider the components outlined in Table 2.

Table 2. Business language and concepts

Concept	Definition/Explanation
Mission	Overriding purpose in line with values or expectations of stakeholders
Vision/Strategic Intent	Long-term aims and aspirations of the company for itself
Objectives and Goals	(Precise) statement of aims or purpose
Strategies	Ways or means in which company objectives are to be achieved and put into effect
Identity	Profile and values communicated by the organization
Image	Immediate set of meanings inferred by an individual in confrontation/response to one or more signals from or about a particular organization at a single point in time
Reputation	An individual's collective representation of past images of an organization (induced through either communication or past experiences) established over time
Stakeholder	Any group or individual that can affect or is affected by achievement of the organization's objectives
Public	People who mobilize themselves against or for the organization on the basis of some common issue or concern to them
Market	A defined group for whom a product is or may be in demand (and for whom an organization creates and maintains products and service offerings)
Issues	An unsettled matter (which is ready for a decision) or a point of conflict between an organization and one or more publics
Communication	Internal and external communication techniques and media used toward internal and external groups or audiences
Integration	The act of coordinating all communications so that the corporate identity is effectively and consistently communicated to internal and external groups, stakeholders, or audiences

Source: Adapted from Cornelissen 2004, 25–26.

Concepts such as mission, vision, objectives and goals, image, strategies, identity, and reputation help in understanding the organizational culture. Asking questions about stakeholders, public, and markets helps in establishing the audience—both internal and external. Reflecting on issues or threats can help define the challenges that might impact strategy, communications, and integration. All these pieces must be perceived as core to developing a strategic communication strategy. Questions an SME could use for a communication audit may include:

- In the past, how have we informed our stakeholders, both internal and external, about our business? What worked? What did not? Why?

- What are our current goals and objectives for our communication strategy? Is it working? Why or why not?

- Does our communication strategy support our overall strategic plan or mission? How well do we integrate and coordinate our communication approaches? What would make it more effective?

- What is our brand, identity, or image, both internally and externally? Are our messages clear and consistent as they pertain to our desired identity or image?

- What is our market? Who are the key audiences in that market? What communication channels does each market segment have access to and use?

- What communication opportunities are we failing to tap and use?

- What environmental or structural factors negatively affect our organization's communication system?

- What type of budget or resources (e.g., human, financial), if any, do we have to build on? What is the cost versus the value added?

Information, Communication, and Technologies Resources

Information, communication, and technologies (ICT) encompass any communication device or application. This comprises a broad spectrum of communication tools from radio, television, and cellular phones to computer and network hardware and software, including the various services and applications they provide. Ondiege (2010) argues that Africa's ICT sector is one of the fastest growing innovations. User or stakeholder participation may be the most dramatic change brought about by ICT in Africa. Accordingly, SMEs not only have to commit financial and human resources to accessing ICT, but they must also more effectively facilitate interaction with their various stakeholders (Tiago and Verissimo 2014). In Africa this interaction is especially pronounced within the social media and mobile technology realms.

Social Media

Social media, sometimes referred to as 'social networking,' is a phenomenon that is transforming the business environment. It facilitates greater creativity, more open communication, and increased knowledge sharing among users (Jagongo and Kinyua 2013). "Real-world social relationships have been migrated to the virtual world, resulting in online communities that bring people together from across the globe" (Tiago and Verissimo 2014, 703). For example, in the marketing world the advent of social media is changing approaches to branding, promotion and advertising, market research, publishing, customer support, and many other aspects that can impact a company's overall performance. This shift encourages more interactions based on digital engagement, which requires SMEs to focus on relationship-based interaction with their customers and other stakeholders (Tiago and Verissimo 2014). From a consumer's perspective, the use of information technologies, especially social media, is perceived to come with benefits such as convenience, efficiency, more product variation and diversity, competitive pricing, and enhanced participation in the consumer process. This has put more pressure on businesses to engage in social networking (Tiago and Verissimo 2014).

A study carried out by Jagongo and Kinyua (2013) found that social media played a role in SMEs' broadening of market access, engaging in competitive pricing, and encouraging innovation. Additionally, social media helped with managing customer relationships through interactions. Figure 3 illustrates the types of social media and their potential benefits.

SMEs must keep in mind that the communication approach and process they choose to use can create or facilitate either opportunities or challenges for entrepreneurship and economic growth (Kristiansen and Ryen 2002). The goal should be for SMEs to use social media effectively, as part of their broader communication strategy, to maximize the effect or impact for positive growth.

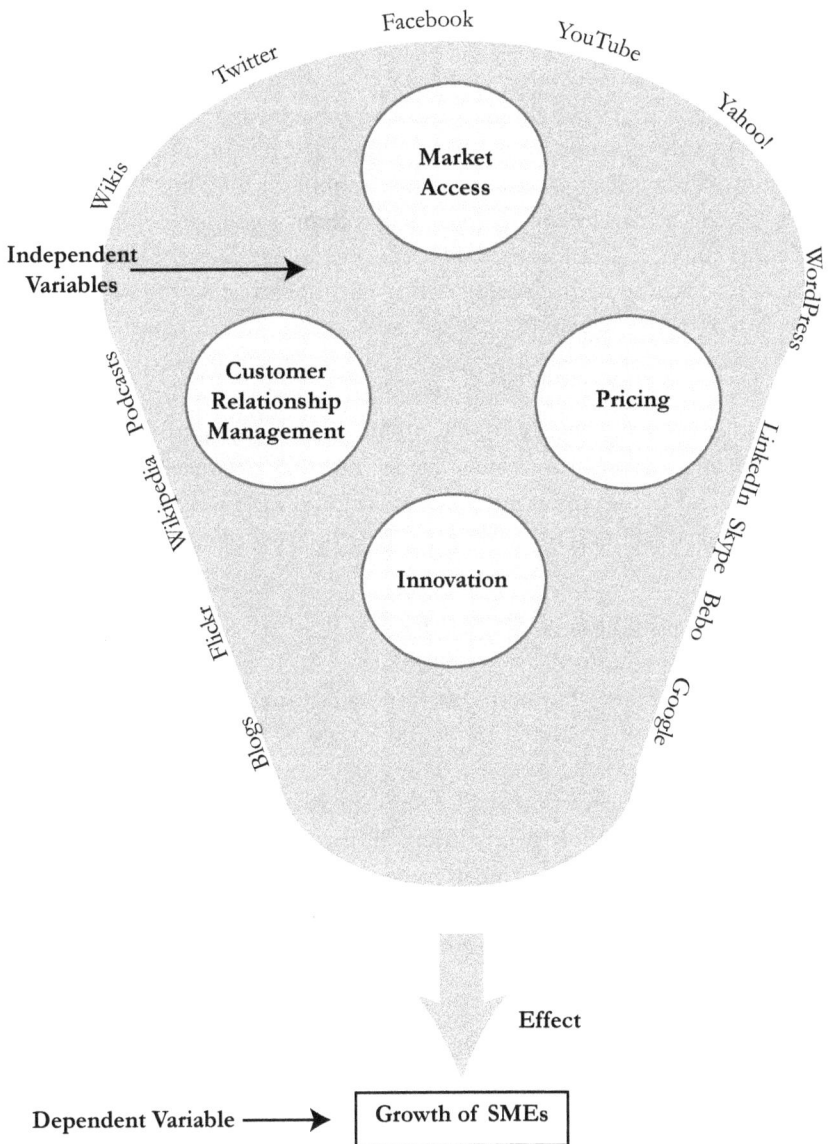

Figure 2: Conceptual framework of ICTs (Source: Adapted from Jagongo and Kinyua 2013)

Mobile Technology

There is an explosive growth of mobile communication in Africa, which has created tremendous advantages for SMEs. No longer are people left behind by the 'digital wave,' but individuals now have access to reliable and efficient technology, even in some of the most remote and resource-poor areas.

Many practitioners would argue that mobile technology has become a key ingredient for addressing poverty in developing countries (Mbogo 2010; Wallis 2011). For SMEs, not only is mobile technology used for informational purposes—whether in marketing, pricing, or other strategic ways—it has also become a tool for facilitating financial transactions. In many parts of Africa, mobile money technology is being used to transact cash and facilitate banking and loans. As suggested by Chief Executive Officer of Kenya Commercial Bank Group Joshua Oigara (2013), "The growth of mobile banking is a natural step towards providing an opportunity to reach mass markets efficiently and fully support financial inclusion. . . . It is a powerful way to deliver savings services to billions of people who have cell phones but no bank accounts.".

ICT, the Trust and Social Capital Factor

In both developed and developing countries, ICT studies have confirmed the value and efficacy of personal or face-to-face contact in establishing and reproducing trust (Urry 2002; Slater and Kwami 2005). But, increasingly, as ICT permeates the SME world in Africa, the issue of trust has been raised repeatedly. The concern is that ICT may increasingly shift communication from more personal or people-focused forms to more impersonal or technology-driven ones. In most African cultures communication has traditionally been viewed from an interpersonal perspective, whereby social capital is frequently gained through family, ethnic, or community networks and trust. The combination of social capital and trust has been called the 'glue' that holds together economic relationships in Africa. In a climate of global uncertainty, this personal trust often sustains the connections that are frequently challenged by distant and complex business transactions (Gabre-Madhin 2001; Molony 2009). If used in an effective and complementary way, ICT may actually help undergird and maintain strong social relations, or what some have called 'socio-technical capital' (Molony 2009).

Other practitioners have studied this issue through the lens of the supply chain network. Effective communication among supply network partners can be beneficial by reducing disruptions, risks, and costs. It can also promote innovation while improving decision-making, competitiveness, and strategic thinking. If not implemented correctly or effectively, however, it can also create vulnerability in business. Communication challenges can range from the lack of technological compatibility across partners to the difficulty of sharing accurate information among dispersed partners. This can lead to distrust within the supply chain network. For example, a stakeholder might question whether an SME has the capacity to produce and deliver a particular order of merchandise in a timely fashion (Kotob and Styger 2012).

The Challenges of Developing a Strategic Communication Approach
For African SMEs the challenges of developing a strategic communication approach are numerous and vary based on many factors—mission, size, location, sector, audience, education, and organizational culture among others. The following section outlines some of these challenges.

Organizational Issues
From an internal perspective, a communication audit in South Africa found that language, literacy, communications skills, human relationships, and attitudes and beliefs were factors that often created barriers in cross-cultural communication settings. Additionally, these factors influenced communication transmission channels and feedback within the organization. For example, sometimes written or electronic channels of communication might exclude valued members of the workforce that may not have access to the technology or may just feel more comfortable with interpersonal methods of communication (Rensburg 1993).

Infrastructure and Capacity Issues
In the attempt to adapt ICT SMEs frequently suffer from weak productive capacity manifested through low domestic and international market coverage. Poor physical and communication infrastructure can compound this problem leading to isolated markets with limited demand (Chowdhury and Wolf 2003). This view is supported by Ozigbo and Ezeaku, whose study of African SMEs found that "most African countries' SMEs are unable to take advantage of economies of scale and capture market opportunities requiring large production runs, standard inputs and consistent standards, often lacking training, market intelligence and the capacity for technological innovation" (2009, 1).

Technological Factors
ICT adoption for SMEs in Africa raises many issues related to technological development. With the growing use of social media as a business tool, for

example, issues of privacy and copyright have to be addressed. The cost of technology also becomes a barrier for SMEs (Jagongo and Kinyua 2013). "SMEs need cost effective and efficient marketing communications mix which are commensurate with their resources. . . . The small business owner should rely on little things that can take their business to greater heights" (Tsikirayi, Muchenje, and Katsidzira 2013, 10).

Monitoring and Evaluation
Like most types of strategic communication initiatives, it is difficult to develop a monitoring and evaluation strategy. At the core of this challenge is the intent of communication strategies—to change behavior. Human behavior is complex, so the indicators we use to measure it may be flawed. Additionally, communication strategies tend to be developed for broad reach, which then makes it challenging to define a specific target audience to assess change. In some business sectors, like agriculture, adoption of ideas may take a long period of time, which can be hard to measure. The cost and the fast nature of ICT implementation and adoption also makes it difficult to measure their impact.

Policy Issues
In many African countries governmental policies have lagged behind ICT adoption. Where this is the case, governments must be encouraged and commit to keeping up with current ICT trends to align policy with practice for SME growth. But it is not just government policy at the macro level that sometimes lags behind. Organizational policies at the micro levels also need to be relevant. For example, research has shown that adoption of appropriate communication practices can influence employees' understanding and commitment to organizational policies and practices, impacting SMEs' growth (Nyamwanza 2014).

Best Practices: The Opportunities Created by Strategic Communication

Despite the challenges, the use of "ICT can provide SMEs with valuable information, increase knowledge, improved performance, improve relationships with customers and suppliers, increase efficiency, reduce cost of production among others" (Akomea-Bonsu and Sampong 2012, 152). Several of these best practices are suggested below.

Taking stock: As outlined earlier in the chapter, taking stock is often a good beginning point. A communication audit or a SWOT analysis is important for all businesses to guide the development of a strategic communication approach that is integrated to maximize impact and growth. This step is central to establishing the organization culture.

Build in, then out: With the increased pressures of globalization, especially the growth of technological capabilities, it is easy to have the various participants within organizations separated or on 'different pages.' Whether it is management, owners, or employees—they must be part of the internal fabric of the business to ensure the rise of the elements critical to maintaining organizational stability and fostering adaptation to changing global landscapes (Peng and Litteljohn 2001). "An organization cannot build relationships externally until it builds them internally" (Niemann 2005, 108). As an SME, what do you want to be known as and what do you want to be known for? These questions must be addressed internally in order to effectively build a strategic communication approach externally.

Diversify and integrate based on audience needs: If you own or are part of a business, you already have diverse stakeholders to target and build your communication strategy around. At the most basic, if you are the only employee, you may have different types of customers defined by many factors—cultural context, language, income, gender, and other indicators. Other SMEs may have both employees and customers. As businesses grow, SMEs may add board members and other stakeholders. Wherever your SME may be in the spectrum of growth, you have to clearly know and define your audience and their particular needs especially when it comes to information and communication strategies. For example, if you have a more rural-based audience, you may have to consider aspects that impact communication— local languages, literacy levels, and infrastructure. This may lead to developing communication focused more on interpersonal aspects, such as face-to-face interaction or network-type approaches through mobile technology, to pass and share information and knowledge.

Establish and maintain trust: Effective communication requires trust. Your audience has to trust you enough to believe your message—whether the communication is personal or impersonal. Trust helps build connections and linkages that facilitate business growth and opportunities for SMEs.

Measure, measure, measure: Monitoring and evaluation can be costly and difficult, but as part of developing strategic communication strategies, SMEs must engage a component of measuring their effectiveness and impact. Indicators may include: number of face-to-face interactions, messages sent via text, number of hits on a site, percentage of readership, or the number of 'likes' on Facebook. Deciding what to measure is complex and may sometimes require external insights or consulting, but it is critical for the growth and sustainability of SMEs. As the saying goes, "One cannot manage what one does not measure" (Eisenberg, Johnson, and Pieterson 2015, 146).

Invest in education and training: Education, whether formal or informal, is critical for growth of SMEs in Africa. In their World Bank–generated survey, Ramachandran and Shah (1999) suggest that individuals that have secondary education or a university degree (or both) tend to have the skills and ability to help their firms grow. The authors confirm that education can provide managerial skills needed for hiring and supervising employees. This ultimately can help generate or sustain employment and maintain retention at higher rates. Thus, business curriculums in the formal education sector must be reviewed to ensure they maintain relevance to supporting SMEs in strategic communication development. At the same time, there is need for informal training for SMEs. Existing and new partnerships are required between the private and public sectors to ensure entrepreneurial training is provided that includes strategic communication as part of the curriculum.

Seek out and use resources: There are many resources that SMEs can seek out for learning. Two that you may want to research are eTransform Africa (www.eTransformAfrica.org) and Strategic Communications Africa Ltd., or Stratcomm (www.stratcomm-africa.com). A program supported by the World Bank, African Development Bank, and the African Union, eTransform Africa identifies and documents best practices in the use of ICT within various economic sectors under the theme 'Transformation Ready.' Stratcomm Africa is a Ghana-based company that provides SMEs with training in appropriate communication strategies and approaches for business growth.

Conclusion: Policy to Support Practice

In summary, policy must be addressed at both the organizational and governmental level. Each SME must adopt the policies that ensure that it can achieve its mission. Governments must also play their part. As highlighted in the eTransform Africa report, "Governments have an important part to play in creating an enabling environment and in acting as a role model and lead client in adopting new innovations and technologies" (World Bank and African Development Bank 2011, 14). In a survey carried out among African SMEs, Ozigbo and Ezeaku (2009) compiled and developed a list of specific policy and practice strategies that SMEs and governments may use as a guide to strengthen strategic communication. At the organizational level, strategy components were outlined and amplified by using concepts such as benchmarking, information sharing, implementation, training, and teaming. At the business and social infrastructure levels, SMEs seemed to emphasize capacity building through learning, networking, and collaboration. Finally, at the policy level, there was a call for dialogue and collaboration to ensure policies align with practice. All these pieces must be on the radar of SMEs in Africa if they are to build an integrated strategic communication system to ensure sustainable growth and impact.

Sources

Akomea-Bonsu, C., and F. Sampong (2012). The Impact of Information and Communication Technologies (ICT) on Small and Medium Scale Enterprises (SMEs) in the Kumasi Metropolis, Ghana, West Africa. *European Journal of Business and Management* 4(20): 152–158.

Argenti, P., R. Howell, and K. Beck (2005). The Strategic Communication Imperative'. *MIT Sloan Management Review*, vol. 46, no. 3, pp. 82-89.

Ariyo, D. (2005). Small Firms Are the Backbone of the Nigerian Economy. African Economic Analysis. http://www.africaeconomicanalysis.org/articles/gen/smallhtm.html (accessed February 15, 2015).

Baker, J. (2008). Why Leaders Fail: When the Best Strategies Can't Get It Done. *BusinessWest* 25(14): 10.

Chowdhury, S., and S. Wolf (2003). Use of ICTs and the Economic Performance of SMEs in East Africa. Discussion Paper No. 2003/06, UNU/WIDER.

Cornelissen, J. (2004). *Corporate Communications: Theory and Practice*. London: Sage.

Eisenberg, E., Z. Johnson, and W. Pieterson (2015). Leveraging Social Networks for Strategic Success. *International Journal of Business Communication* 52(1): 143–154.

Gabre-Madhin, E. Z. (2001). *Market Institutions, Transaction Costs, and Social Capital in the Ethiopian Grain Market*, Research Report No. 124, Washington, DC: International Food Policy Research Institute. http://ageconsearch.umn.edu/bitstream/16540/1/rr010124.pdf (accessed on February 25, 2015)

Hallahan, K., D. Holtzhausen, B. van Ruler, D. Vercic, and K. Sriramesh (2007). Defining Strategic Communication. *International Journal of Strategic Communication* 1(1): 3–35.

Jagongo, A. and C. Kinyua (2013). The Social Media and Entrepreneurship Growth: A New Business Communication Paradigm among SMEs in Nairobi. *International Journal of Humanities and Social Science* 3(10): 213–227.

Jarzabkowski, P., J. Balogun, and D. Seidl (2007). Strategizing: The Challenges of a Practice Perspective. *Human Relations* 60(1): 5–27.

Kristiansen, S., and A. Ryen (2002). Enacting Their Business Environments: Asian Entrepreneurs in East Africa. *African and Asian Studies* 1(3): 165–186.

Kotob, F., and L. Styger (2012). 'A Comparison of Supply Integration and End-to-End Communication Theory and Practice—An Australian Perspective. Proceeding of 19th International Business Research Conference 2012. http://dx.doi.org/10.2139/ssrn.2174202 (accessed March 12, 2015).

Magagula, J. M. (2008). Communication Strategies Aimed at Improving the Success Rate of Small to Medium Business Enterprises. Master's thesis, University of Zululand, South Africa.

Oigara, J. (2013) MFW4A-Making Finance Work for Africa 'New Mobile Banking Service Launched in Kenya.': http://www.mfw4a.org/news/news-details/browse/4/article/410/new-mobile-banking-service-launched-in-kenya.html. (Retrieved on February 28, 2015).

Mbogo, M. (2010). The Impact of Mobile Payments on the Success and Growth of Micro-Business: The Case of M-Pesa in Kenya. *The Journal of Language, Technology & Entrepreneurship in Africa* 2(1): 182–203.

Mody, B. (2003). *International and Development Communication: A 21st-Century Perspective.* Thousand Oaks, CA: Sage.

Molony, T. (2009). Carving a Niche: ICT, Social Capital, and Trust in the Shift from Personal to Impersonal Trading in Tanzania. *Information Technology for Development* 15(4): 283–301.

Niemann, I. (2005). Strategic Integrated Communication Implementation: Towards a South African Conceptual Model. PhD diss., University of Pretoria, South Africa.

Nyamwanza, T. (2014). An Analysis of Communication Approaches Used by SMEs in Zimbabwe. *European Centre for Research Training and Development* 2(1): 39–50.

Ondiege, P. (2010). Mobile Banking in Africa: Taking the Bank to the People. African Development Bank, *Africa Economic Brief* 1(8).

Ozigbo, N., and P. Ezeaku (2009). Adoption of Information and Communication Technologies to the Development of Small and Medium Scale Enterprises (SMEs) in Africa. *Journal of Business and Administrative Studies* 1(1): 1–19.

Peng, W. and D. Litteljohn (2001). Organisational Communication and Strategy Implementation—A Primary Inquiry. *International Journal of Contemporary Hospitality Management* 13(7): 360–363.

Ramachandran, V., and M. Shah (1999). Minority Entrepreneurs and Firm Performance in Sub-Saharan Africa. RPED Paper no. 080. Washington, DC: The World Bank.

Rensburg, R. (1993). Societal vs. Organizational Culture: Toward a Cross-Cultural Communication Model for South African Organizations. *Intercultural Communication Studies* 3(1): 75–90.

Slater, D., and J. Kwami (2005). *Embeddedness and Escape: Internet and Mobile Use as Poverty Reduction Strategies in Ghana* (No. 4). London: Information Society Research Group.

Tsikirayi, C., B. Muchenje, and Z. Katsidzira (2013). Impact of Integrated Marketing Communications Mix (IMCM) in Small to Medium Enterprises (SMEs) in Zimbabwe as a Marketing Tool. *Research in Business & Economics Journal* 7: 167.

Thomas, G., and K. Stephens (2015). An Introduction to Strategic Communication. *International Journal of Business Communication* 52(1): 3–11.

Tiago, M. T., and J. M. Verissimo (2014). Digital Marketing and Social Media: Why Bother? *Business Horizons* 57: 703–708.

Urry, J. (2002). Mobility and Proximity. *Sociology* 36(2): 255–274.

Wallis, C. (2011). Mobile Phones without Guarantees: The Promises of Technology and the Contingencies of Culture. *New Media and Society* 13(3): 471–485.

White, S. (1999). *The Art of Facilitating Participation*. New Delhi: Sage.

World Bank and African Development Bank (2012). *The Transformational Use of Information and Communication Technologies in Africa*. Executive Report. Washington, DC: eTransform Africa.

IT'S ALL IN THE FAMILY: FAMILY AGRIBUSINESSES IN AFRICA

Njeri Gakonyo

Introduction

Most of us are not conscious of it, but family business abounds around the world, contributing between 70% and 90% of global gross domestic product. Some estimates indicate that 65% to 80% of all businesses are rooted in family relationships. Notably, the vast majority of family businesses are small and medium enterprises (SMEs). In agriculture in particular, family farms predominate in both developing and developed countries, prompting the Food and Agriculture Organization of the United Nations to declare 2014 the Year of Family Farming,[1] but families are also involved in input and output markets. In terms of performance, family business is well represented: 40% of the Fortune 500 are family businesses, and indices that track their performance show better results than conventional business. For example, the United Kingdom Family Business Index outperforms the FTSE All-Share by 40%, and the United States shows similar trends. Over time, this type of enterprise has grown in importance, drawing attention to the unique needs and opportunities family businesses present, spawning supportive services in response.

---

1   See http://www.fao.org/family-farming-2014/en/.

Recognizing the specific needs of these enterprises, in 2014 Making Markets Matter (MMM) introduced a session on family business, and the topic drew significant interest from participants. Those representing family businesses as owners and managers shared their backgrounds and experiences, highlighting how family involvement had helped to start and continue the businesses. At the same time, they were keen to hear about some old—and new—ideas and solutions that could strengthen their businesses and boost their performance.

This chapter reflects on some of the issues that surfaced in our conversations. The topic is of special interest to those involved in a family business, and they will readily recognize their businesses on the following pages, which provide insights to help unlock the potential of their business. At the same time, the chapter may well reveal some useful information for others interested in this topic, which lies squarely at the intersection of business and human relationships.

What is Family Business?

Although family businesses are common, there is no one universally accepted definition. Some prefer the term "family owned business" (FOB) to indicate that the stake-holding aspect is fundamental. In this chapter we follow Poza's (2004) criteria to determine whether yours is a family business:

- **Ownership:** two or more family members hold a significant stake;
- **Influence:** family members participate in the board and/or in management;
- **Involvement criteria:** the business recognizes family relationships when deciding who may be involved, e.g., it accepts investment or senior management only from the family;
- **Long-term view:** the business considers the possibility of continuing to the next generation of the family.

Considering that our focus is on Africa in particular, the term "family" means not just the nuclear family (parents and their children), but extended family as well: relations at different levels, by both blood and marriage, including polygamous connections. The other factor that matters in defining family for the purpose of business is ethnic culture. In some contexts, a family's obligation to ensure employment or income for every member is quite strong. Stories abound of relatives fully expecting your business to find a role for them, almost as a right.

N. Gakonyo

Family Business in Africa

In comparison to other world regions, there is relatively little understanding of how family business operates in Africa. Yet, there is little doubt that families operating a business are an important feature of the continent's economic landscape. *Forbes* magazine has listed Africa's largest family businesses, while large consulting firms have specialized family business offerings. Table 1 lists some of Africa's largest and best-known businesses in which families are involved at board level.

Table 1. Large African family businesses

Business info	Family and involvement	Country
Pick 'n Pay founded in 1966 *Industry:* grocery retail *Size:* 800 stores, $5.6 billion turnover	Ackerman family holds 53% stake	South Africa
Dantata founded in 1910 *Industry:* oil exploration, manufacturing, banking and finance, import and export, farming, merchandising, commodity trading *Size:* over $300 million turnover	Dantata family in top management	Nigeria
METL Group founded in 1960 *Industry:* textile and soap manufacturing, financial services, retail, petroleum marketing *Size:* over $1 billion turnover	Dewji family in top management and on board	Tanzania
Madhvani Group founded in 1918 *Industry:* sugar, hotels, tea estates, construction, insurance, distribution, owning and running Kakira Airport *Size:* asset base over $400 million	Madhvani family in top management	Uganda
Kenyatta family businesses founded in the late 1960s *Industry:* land holdings, hotels, dairy, media, banking *Size:* between $500 million and $1 billion	Kenyatta family in top management and on board	Kenya

Around the world, the two areas in which family business is most likely to succeed are services and food. Family enterprise is likely to become more important in agribusiness in Africa for a couple of key reasons. First, as long as the financial sector continues to consider agriculture too risky to fund, the most widely available alternative is family resources. Second, Africa's current enormous youth bulge has governments hurrying to seek occupational opportunities all over the economy, but agriculture presents the greatest potential. The World Bank estimates the agribusiness market in Africa to reach $1 trillion by 2030, given the growth of populations, incomes, urbanization, and export markets. Over two-thirds of Sub-Saharan Africa's population is involved in agriculture, mostly in smallholdings. This means that most young people are getting firsthand farming experience (even if they may aspire to leave the farm altogether). Efforts to improve young people's engagement in agriculture will often call for their family's involvement as guardians, financiers or underwriters, mentors, and coaches. Moreover, as the subdivision of already small farms becomes increasingly unviable, families may seek to integrate backward into input supply or forward into processing in order to strengthen their overall economic prospects. As African agriculture modernizes and becomes more sophisticated, if the current trend of SME dominance continues, those SMEs are likely to be family-owned and run.

One broad-brush feature of family business in Africa is a **high degree of informality**. Largely due to the developing country context, most of these businesses are SMEs that are not formal entities. The environment for business has little rule of law, government bureaucracy is maze-like and inefficient, corruption is rampant (extortion is a significant business expense), modern infrastructure is extremely limited, and supportive services (e.g., finance) are biased against SMEs. Table 2 summarizes some ways in which African FOBs are informal compared with those of industrialized nations.

In general, informality may be useful and necessary when a business is at start-up stage or operating on a small scale. The larger the business gets, however, the more will informality put it at a disadvantage. Therefore, although structures can feel constraining, African family businesses that aspire to reach the heights need to learn how to become formal in their operations. This requires changes in mindset as well as acquiring new skills (and unlearning bad habits) to function in new ways. The rewards include reduced costs of avoiding the law (including bribes to regulatory officials), increased confidence in the business from financiers and an ability to expand to new locations due to effective structures.

Table 2. Comparison of African and developed economies' FOBs

Comparison	FOBs in Africa	FOBs in developed economies
Ownership and direction	Founder is sole owner, decision maker, manager, and comptroller	Founder and spouse own Often have a board of directors or advisors
Legal status	Most are informal and unregistered, but a few may be registered with government Operate without license	Most are formal and registered A few may be unregistered, but hide from government Can only operate with required licenses
Source of capital	Most start with own family equity capital Rarely start with debt from formal financial institutions May borrow from relatives	Most mix little own equity with debt Most secure debt from financial entities by qualifying Debt may rarely be secured from relatives
Production activities	Founder in charge with unpaid assistance from family members	Founder in charge but may employ paid assistance
Distribution of dividends	Founder solely controls profits No written record of dividend	Founder controls profits except where there are other shareholders Keep detailed accounts for tax and banking purposes

Source: adopted from Gupta *et al.* (2010)

Box: Tuskys, an East African Family Business (www.tuskys.com)

Tuskys is a 34-year-old retail business that has become a household name in Kenya and even expanded into East Africa. With a chain of 52 outlets in numerous towns around Kenya (ranging in size from small convenience stores to large supermarkets) and more than 6,000 employees, the brand is now the second largest retail chain in the Great Lakes region. In recent years, through stories in the media, the family business aspects of the group have emerged.

Business origins: In the 1980s Joram Kamau had a small shop known as Magic, which sold mattresses in Rongai (near Nakuru in the Rift Valley). Joram had a special relationship with a business across the street, Nakuru Mattresses, through which Magic was able to run a low-price strategy. Joram had five sons, who later joined him in the business. This family presence made it possible to expand the business to central Nakuru and Nairobi through a subsidiary called Tusker Mattresses Limited—revamping the brand into the name Tuskys in 2007. To the low-price strategy the supermarket added strategic locations in busy spots such as bus terminals and densely packed neighborhoods. In 2000 the brothers merged Magic and Tusker Mattresses and proceeded to develop the business into a formidable enterprise with 57 branches in Kenya and Uganda and over $236 million (KES 20 billion) in turnover by 2010, second only to Nakumatt (previously Nakuru Mattresses) in retail. Joram died in 2002, leaving the business to his five sons and two daughters. He passed on the original Magic shop in Rongai to his brother, who subsequently grew it into the Naivas supermarket chain, now also one of the country's top retail groups.

Family involvement: All five brothers are involved in the day-to-day running of Tusksys: first-born John Kago (board chair), second Samuel Gatei, third Stephen Mukuha (holding the managing director position from 2001 to 2014), fourth Yusuf Mugweru (director of sales and marketing), and fifth George Gachwe (currently the managing director). All seven siblings sit on the board and there are no nonfamily board members. In terms of shareholding, except for Kago, each brother owns a 17.5% stake (totaling 70%) in Orakam, the holding company of Tuskys. Kago and the two sisters share the remaining 30%.

How they became successful: Although Joram's business was working well, when his sons joined, they clearly brought fresh energy and ideas that drove major expansion. The company's vision is to become "a successful brand on every street and corner." The family has demonstrated astute business acumen by targeting a large and growing demographic, establishing related businesses that integrated into the Tuskys business model, and managing the business well enough (a broad product offering, innovation, and customer loyalty tactics) to expand into the region. There seems to be room for improvement, however, as Tuskys profitability compares poorly with another retail chain, publicly owned Uchumi supermarkets.

Hitting rough waters: Indications that all was not well in the Tuskys empire surfaced around 2012 with newspaper reports of court matters relating to the business (after arbitration efforts had failed). Intercompany dealings with the related businesses became problematic, leading to major disputes between family members. "The cosy business relationship between Tuskys and the brothers' private interests worked well as long as everyone appeared to be getting a fair share and everything was on the table." Unhealthy and underhanded practices eroded trust between family members, in particular claims of fraudulent transfer of funds from Tuskys to the other companies and breach of agreements on strategy (such as whether to acquire versus lease premises). In addition, the siblings argued over the appointment of a senior nonfamily member to a director-level position as well as who should be listed on critical company bank accounts as signatories.

By August 2014, the family disputes culminated in six of the siblings engineering a leadership change, removing third-born Stephen Mukuha from the managing director position and replacing him with fifth-born George Gachwe after a business acquisition attempt failed; Mukuha remains on the board and still has some executive involvement. Altogether, the various issues resulted in several family members being suspended from the business, physical altercation between two brothers, leadership changes, some business upheaval, and court cases that damaged the business's public image (previously, the company had managed to keep its affairs well under wraps). Nevertheless, the business remains a fairly strong going concern.

We can only try to infer the factors that gave rise to the problems: there seem to have been weaknesses in business governance—in both structures and practices. Why was it possible, or even easy, for intercompany transactions to be somewhat opaque? Was communication or conduct within the board insufficiently effective at managing the issues? How come the family bonds were unable to overcome the distrust?

Sources: Business Daily (2014). Tuskys MD Replaced after Failed Ukwala Takeover. August 11. http://www.businessdailyafrica.com/Corporate-News/Tuskys-MD-replaced-after-failed-Ukwala-takeover/-/539550/2415972/-/n98dvg/-/index.html.

The East African (2012). Trouble in the Empire: An Inside Look at Tuskys Supermarkets Family Drama. April 28. http://www.theeastafrican.co.ke/news/Trouble-in-the-empire-An-inside-look-at-Tusky-family-drama/-/2558/1395600/-/v4bb53/-/index.html. Wikipedia. http://en.wikipedia.org/wiki/Tuskys.

Why is Family Business Likely to be More Successful than Other Business Types?

As mentioned earlier, family businesses outperform other business types around the world. From the Tuskys story it is noteworthy that three of Kenya's top retail chains are family affairs. Indeed, it was when Joram Kamau's sons joined the business that it received the boost to become a force to be reckoned with—and it still is despite the rocky times. For a start, a business that operates for the family's sake tends to have **deeper commitment** to making the business work. Since family members often feel that ensuring stable, rising income is a core reason why the business exists in the first place, they will go the extra mile to run it well and make it succeed.[2] At the same time, when the community knows that yours is a family business, you have an incentive not to fail, since that endangers the family's reputation. Other family members feel they have a stake in your business success because you share a lineage and/or name.

If conventional business struggles for financing, family business has **access to funds** from relatives who do not impose high requirements: the test of whether you are a worthwhile risk is easy and often unrelated to how strong a businessperson you are. If you approach a bank or private equity firm, often there is a long application and due diligence process for which you need to have established structures and even a track record. In contrast, family members will give or loan funds based on what they know of you as a person, a business proposal that sounds reasonable (even if it is untested or would not stand up to scrutiny), or the degree to which they see the business as an opportunity for you to thrive. One or a few conversations may be sufficient for family members to transfer their money to you for the business. In some cultures, this kind of support is actually an obligation—making it even easier to tap family for funds. For all these reasons, financing from family is often the kindest for startups or struggling businesses. The business owner, for her part, may be less likely to be reckless with resources that have come from people with whom she shares a family bond versus a bank or unrelated investor.[3]

---

2   The 2013 Family Business Survey (USA) found that family employees work an average of 20.6 years in the business versus 4.6 years for people working in nonfamily business (http://smallbiztrends.com/2014/01/what-you-can-learn-from-family-businesses.html).

3   The other significant source of capital for business in Africa is the local community, such as members of a church or women's group (see Khavul et al., 2009).

Moreover, when family members put their money into a business, they tend to be more patient in expecting returns. A father, brother, aunt, or cousin is usually willing to give substantial cash (or other in-kind investment) without stipulating the kind of return he or she expects and within what time frame. Indeed, often their investment stays undocumented in the business and may end up being a grant to the enterprise. Over time, they may remain completely silent business partners or keep up with the business's ups and downs as supportive or encouraging voices. When you approach them for re-investment, unless you have really messed up, they will seriously consider giving you more money on the basis of the family relationship. This kind of **patient capital** allows the business more latitude to take risks, to innovate, and to work out the kinks in running the business—all of which can take time before yielding results. Many conventional businesses struggle because investors are demanding, affording little breathing room for the entrepreneur to endure through rough times. The family business therefore has a significant advantage in this respect. One major advantage of nonpatient capital, however, is that it enforces the discipline the entrepreneur needs to avoid excessive risks, wasteful ventures, or dubious practices. Family members typically demand little oversight (they do not ask to see accounts, business strategy, or marketing plans, which would show how seriously the business is being run), enabling those in the business to be less careful.

One particularly valuable feature of family business is a high degree of **trust** among those involved, whether investors or board members or family employees. Most of us trust a family member more than someone outside the family, because he or she has family obligations toward us, we share core values, and we already know his or her strengths and weaknesses. We expect the family bond to mean that they are less likely to do things that will harm the business and are willing to go beyond the call of duty. The Tuskys story is remarkable for the kind of sibling bonds that enabled the business to grow to its current large size. The strains now emerging may be more related to the difficulties of managing a large, multifaceted enterprise. In contrast, nonfamily members need to prove themselves first, before attaining a high level of trust. Of course, this trust in family can be unwarranted or mistaken. For example, many of us have experience of family members who bring an attitude of entitlement to their involvement, expecting gains for little or no contribution.[4] At least with nonfamily members the expectation

---

4   In Africa, cultural norms often dictate that better-off family members should support financially weaker relatives. Because these family bonds often mean you are expected

of performance in exchange for benefits (such as employment income or dividends) is clear from the outset. The commitment, patient capital, and trust factors in family business together help make it a more **stable** and **resilient** enterprise than other forms of business.

Making Family Business Work Takes Effort

Understanding the difference family involvement makes to running a business is critical. One widely known model, developed by Renato Tagiuri and John Davis at Harvard Business School in the 1970s,[5] depicts the setting as three interlocking spheres of operation: the family, the business ownership (shareholders) together with direction (board), and the business management (see Figure 1).

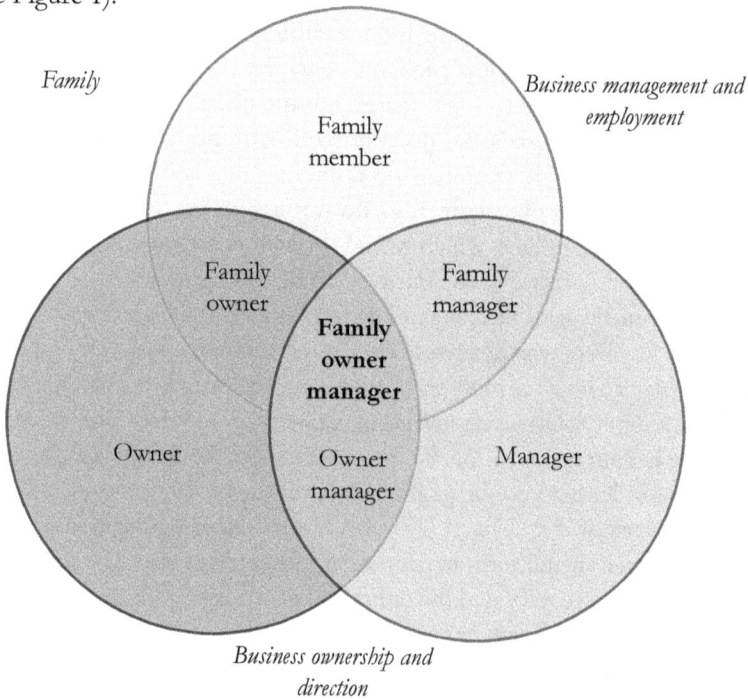

Family

Business management and employment

Family member

Family owner

Family manager

Family owner manager

Owner

Owner manager

Manager

Business ownership and direction

Figure 1. Three-circle model of the family business system
(Source: http://www.paradigmassociates.us/family-business/life-cycle-issues.php)

---

to offer relatives employment in your business (whether they are qualified or not; whether they have a strong work ethic or not), the sense of entitlement can run high.

5   See http://johndavis.com/three-circle-model-of-the-family-business-system/.

It is important to **recognize the values, interests, and expectations of each segment**. Does a family shareholder (not involved in running the business) expect actual financial returns? Does the family manager understand that the company needs to run on business values, rather than paying excessive attention to family needs? Since business operates in a competitive space, there are other companies in the same market that may not have family concerns and may therefore have an edge over yours, if you fail to emphasize business principles. The manager who does not belong to the family may feel quite vulnerable if family members and issues keep taking priority. Managers need to take the time to speak to people in each segment to understand their motivations and concerns. This knowledge will help to decide where and how to clarify matters, making your expectations clear for each role and allaying fears when necessary.

There are key fundamental differences between the family and business entities: each has its own norms (ways of doing things), membership rules, value types, interests, motivations, and organizational structures. Thus, whereas in a family the value of caring for others may be paramount, in business the main value is delivering results. Because of the ways these two spheres differ, involvement in both the family and the business **needs firm, appropriate boundaries** between the two. These boundaries are in essence rules or guidelines that stipulate what is appropriate in which context. For example, all movement of money in the business needs to be documented, even if it is a family member (including the owner) moving it. Note how the lack of transparency in intercompany accounts in the Tuskys case triggered disputes that affected the business. Another tricky area is setting rules for who can give instructions to company employees. The informality of family business in Africa often means that family members outside the company freely commandeer employee time or company resources. This kind of practice can mushroom into a major problem so the business leadership needs to set and enforce rules.

Problems can also arise because the same individuals have to fulfill obligations in family and business, and poor boundaries mean that issues from one sphere carry over into the other. Again, finances are one major area of spillover: business owners need to ensure that there is separation of funds that belong to the business and funds of the family. For instance, many family SME chief executive officers (CEOs) do not pay themselves a salary, but dip into the till periodically based on household needs. This practice can cause a great deal of confusion and impact business cash flow. Families typically resolve family–business interface issues through power and politics, but policies and purpose are also needed. For instance, in the Tuskys story, clear company policies and adequate oversight of transactions with related businesses could have helped avoid the damaging disputes.

The distinction between owners or directors and managers also causes many dilemmas for family business.[6] Even in many conventional businesses it is difficult for directors and shareholders feeling the urge to dabble in day-to-day managerial affairs to keep to their governance and oversight roles. This tendency can be worse in a family because of the sense that everyone must pull together to make things work. **Giving due respect** to each role is critical, making expectations clear and holding each person accountable for his or her role. A sensitive issue is that of automatically making family members managers even if they lack the qualifications or skills to be good managers for the sake of the business. Best practice recommends putting family members through the necessary business training and experience before giving them major responsibilities. The family member running the business needs to set performance and promotion standards that apply to everyone or risk losing the talented nonfamily employees who do not see a future for themselves in the company. At the same time, putting burdensome expectations on family employees or not giving them adequate compensation may prod them to leave.

In the African cultural environment where informal business prevails, there is a need to **learn boundary-setting and enforcing skills.** Although family can be a source of strength for the business, it needs to offer support in ways that do not cause problems for the company.

The following two subsections discuss two critical functional issues for family business: communication and succession. Poor practices on these two issues often plague family business, dimming the business success. Once you can clarify and instill good practice in these two areas, you increase your chances of driving your business to great achievements.

---

6   Family is often nervous about bringing nonfamily people into owner or director positions, fearing their influence on decision-making and tending to prefer virtual sycophants. The more a business seeks to operate as an independent entity, the more important it becomes to have fairly independent-minded people who can hold family accountable.

Communication

With regard to communication, the big danger is creating two classes of employees based on whether they are members of the family or not. Sometimes family members know much more about the business than their nonfamily colleagues. This creates a sense of unfairness among nonfamily employees, which may lead to damaging resentment. Managers should emphasize the need for **transparency** and **sharing of knowledge** with employees based on their role within the company, not their family affiliation. It is also important to avoid giving confidential family information to nonfamily employees. Each facet of the three circles needs its own communication structures and channels as Table 3 suggests.

Table 3. Communication structures and channels

Family	Business management	Business ownership and direction
Family meeting—everyone	Management meetings	Shareholders' annual general meeting
Family council—selected representatives	Department meetings	
	Staff meetings	Board and board committee meetings
Spell out channels of communication	Staff get-togethers	Spell out board's scope of responsibility
Conflict resolution mechanisms		Spell out shareholder exit options and procedures

Whereas it is easy to find advice and examples for the business communication structures and channels, creativity and commonsense are needed to design similar tools that suit the family. Overall, a strongly **positive** (willingness to share information and constructive opinions) and **disciplined** (with an appropriate mix of transparency and confidentiality) **communication culture** can smooth business activities greatly.

Succession

Lack of clarity on succession from one generation to the next is the major reason why family businesses fail to endure beyond the life of the founder. Worldwide, on average a founder will run a business for over 20 years and then exit (either by leaving the business or dying). But only 30% of family businesses successfully manage transition to the second generation, while a mere 15% successfully pass on to the third generation. Most founders procrastinate or are outright reluctant to plan their replacement. Without a clear, well-communicated succession plan, departure of the founder results in a power vacuum, which can trigger all kinds of negative emotions and attempts to gain control. Succession in polygamous families can be an additional challenge made worse when the business leader dies without leaving a will. Ogundele et al. (2012) report that in Nigeria, a founder's promising child may hold back on devoting much energy to the business, fearing the many other children's claims to business positions or fortunes. The uncertainty surrounding an opaque succession can cost the business valuable employees' time, attention, and effort, ultimately negatively affecting the bottom line.

There are several options available to a founder upon leaving the business:

- Wind up the company: sell the assets, pay off creditors, and issue the remaining funds to principals;
- Sell the company to employees or outsiders;
- Retain family ownership into the next generation but keep family out of management; or
- Retain family ownership and management control.

The first two options may be useful if a founder feels that the family is unable to keep the business going well due to either inability or lack of interest. Many in farming find that their children want to leave the rural areas altogether, and it is better to plan for this outcome than to leave it unaddressed.[7] The third option recognizes that nonfamily may be better at managing the business. In the Tuskys story, the level of distrust reached the point at which some siblings demanded the company fill the managing director position from outside the family. The last succession option outlined above is viable if founder and family are in agreement about family interests, motivations, and—most importantly—capability to carry on steering the business. If eligible family members outnumber the available management positions, there needs to be real clarity about qualifications to occupy those positions.

---

7   The thorny issue here may be a family's attachment to the land, especially if there are family graves.

For the founder, selection of a successor for the company's helm involves **identifying real leadership** qualities among the candidates. If possible, it is also highly useful to have your chosen successor(s) gain experience outside the company. Founders need to **tap the advice and wisdom of others** who know about generational transitions. As decisions are being made, it is **critical to communicate** key issues and procedures to both family and nonfamily in order to minimize power struggles and uncertainty. Once it is time for the founder to **leave**, he or she should endeavor to do so **gracefully**. Avoid micromanaging your successors or even hanging on beyond the value you can give to the company, particularly because the new generation will have ideas and talents of their own. This often means that you find other interests to pursue and accord your successors the freedom to run company strategy and affairs. Usually, they will need your sound voice of experience from time to time.

Women in Family Business

Women's involvement in family business has interesting differences from other kinds of enterprises, with both advantages and disadvantages. On the plus side, women who participate in the family business enjoy greater flexibility since the family may be more understanding of their needs such as childcare. For example, the business may not insist that she show up to work at eight in the morning and stay in the office until closing time. Moreover, because the family bond matters, women are more likely to rise to the top of the business than in nonfamily establishments: in the Fortune 500, 25% of CEOs in FOBs are women compared with only 3% in nonfamily businesses. Malmsey Rangaka, CEO and co-founder of M'hudi Wines, a family business profiled below, was a visionary who saw the wine business possibilities, providing the drive to create and build a successful family enterprise. Also noteworthy is that women-led FOBs can be quite successful: one U.S. study found that women-led family businesses consistently outperform their male-led peers.[8]

The downside of being a woman in a family business has a number of facets. Families have a tendency to value women's contribution less than

---

8   National Association of Women Business Owners (NAWBO; USA): http://nawbo.org/content_12864.cfm. There are indications that women's leadership style and use of resources yield better results.

men's. It could be that she is employed but her remuneration is lower, or that her ideas carry less weight than her male relatives, or even that her involvement is considered informal (yet it adds real value to the business). Many female spouses put a great deal of time and energy into developing a business from the beginning but are never documented as co-owners or remunerated. Moreover, as Malmsey indicates, women need to be extra-careful about drawing boundaries between their family and business roles. In many cases, women's technical skills are not taken seriously and they are relegated to soft-skill roles. One wonders why it is only the brothers who are engaged in executive roles at Tuskys, whereas the sisters only sit on the board. Also, depending on the culture, women may display strong talent and results, but because they are female they are never considered for the company's top positions—only the men are (even if they are less deserving).

Box: M'hudi Wines, a Successful South African Family Business

M'hudi winery near Stellenbosch in the Western Cape has been the subject of a MMM case study and has remained greatly supportive of the training experience. The Rangaka family ventured into wine-making, establishing the first black-owned winery in South Africa, and built the business into an award-winning set of products that feature in markets in the United States, Europe, and Africa. In a 2012 interview with the business chief executive officer and cofounder, Mamsley Rangaka said family business means keeping the lines clear.

"[Question:] You run the business with your husband and children. What advice can you give to other family run businesses? Is it challenging or does it make things easier?

"[Ms. Rangaka:] It is onerous to be in a family business, particularly as CEO like me. I have to herd a team—I use that word deliberately—that tends to see you in a dual capacity. You have to be careful to ensure that the discipline of business does not get misinterpreted to be personal 'maternal' censure. With your husband involved there is the constant line you have to tread between asserting the claims of your office and maintaining the balance that allows the love affair to continue.

"Succession planning is another issue. If you go by primogeniture [the right of succession by a firstborn child over siblings] and the eldest is incapable or busy elsewhere you then have to break traditional ranks to build up a younger sibling. If it happens that the younger is a daughter all sorts of other issues come to bedevil the matter."

Source: http://www.howwemadeitinafrica.com/entrepreneur-watch-how-to-make-it-in-the-wine-industry/18979/

Overall, most women-owned businesses can attest to the great difficulties they encounter in getting the attention of customers, financiers, government, or other stakeholders. As long as the face of the business is a woman, the quality, reliability, and prospects seem lower to the outside world, irrespective of the actual, objective value.

For women in family businesses, taking advantage of the opportunities while overcoming the negative aspects requires creativity and persistence. The most important aspect is **changing the family's mindset** toward women. Encouragingly, there are anecdotal stories of a patriarchal founder who fully intended to hand over the business to a son, but then changed his mind once he realized that a daughter was more talented or invested and therefore more likely to lead and maintain success.

Family Business Can be Rewarding!

Ultimately, family business can be a highly enjoyable and fulfilling experience, delivering much fruit to customers and family alike. But achieving this result does not come by default: family businesspeople need to be deliberate and explicit about setting and enforcing healthy boundaries between the three spheres. The family can be a major asset to the business if you foster a positive, disciplined culture so that family members' involvement is constructive for the business.

Sources

Brown, Carolyn M. 7 Rules for Avoiding Conflicts of Interest in a Family Business. http://www.inc.com/guides/201102/7-rules-of-conduct-for-family-businesses.html.

Family Firm Institute Inc. Global Data Points. http://www.ffi.org/?page=globaldatapoints.

Family Owned Business and Communication. http://smallbusiness.chron.com/family-owned-business-communication-3165.html.

Gersick, Kelin, John A. Davis, Marion McCollom Hampton, and Ivan Lansberg (1977). *Generation to Generation: Life Cycles of the Family Business*. Harvard Business Review Press.

Goldsmith, Marshal (2009). Why Entrepreneurs Sabotage the Succession Process. *Harvard Business Review,* October 8. http://blogs.hbr.org/2009/10/why-entrepreneurs-sabotage-the/.

Guptaa, Vipin, Nancy Levenburgb, Lynda Moorec, Jaideep Motwanib, and Thomas V. Schwarzd (2010). Family Business in Sub-Saharan Africa Versus the Middle East. *Journal of African Business* 11(2).

Huebsch, Russell. The Advantages of Having a Family Council in a Family Owned Business. http://smallbusiness.chron.com/advantages-having-family-council-family-owned-business-34598.html

Khavul, Susanna, Garry D. Bruton, and Eric Wood (2009, November). Informal Family Business in Africa. *Entrepreneurship Theory and Practice*, 1219–1238.

Manchester Business School and the Cyprus International Institute of Management (2006). *The UK Family Business PLC Economy Study*. Institute for Family Business (UK).

Michaud, Laura. Family Business Communication. http://www.smallbusinessnotes.com/small-business-resources/family-business-communication.html#ixzz31mRO2glQ.

National Association of Women Business Owners. Women Playing a Larger Role in Family-Owned Businesses. http://nawbo.org/content_12864.cfm.

Nsehe, Mfonobong (2014). The 10 Leading Family Businesses in Africa. *Forbes*, January 8.

Ogundele, OLK, AA Idris, K.A. Ahmed-Ogundipe (2012). Entrepreneurial Succession Problems in Nigeria's Family Businesses: A Threat to Sustainability. *European Scientific Journal* 8(7).

Partners for Small Business Excellence. Family-Owned Business Success: Leveraging Advantages and Mastering Challenges. http://www.bobcarr.com/Smallbizpartners/success/XIIarticles/family.html.

Poza, Ernesto J. (2004). *Family Business*. Mason: South-Western.

Small Business Trends (2014). What You Can Learn from Family Businesses. Jan 16. http://smallbiztrends.com/2014/01/what-you-can-learn-from-family-businesses.html.

Rivers, Wayne. What Do Family Members Want? http://www.familybusinessinstitute.com/index.php/volume-4-articles/what-do-family-members-want.html.

World Bank (2013, March). *Growing Africa: Unlocking the Potential of Agribusiness*.

Wuorio, Jeff (1998). *The Succession Crisis*. Success Holdings Company, LLC.

GENDER AND AGRIBUSINESS ENTREPRENEURSHIP IN AFRICA

Linley Chiwona-Karltun and Krisztina Zita Tihanyi

One explicit goal of this volume is to shed light on the ways in which running a small and medium enterprise (SME) in Africa is different from operating SMEs in other parts of the world. This picture would not be complete without a look at the influence of gender—and gender relations—in agripreneurship.[1] Succinctly defined by the Food and Agriculture Organization of the United Nations (FAO), "gender roles are the 'social definition' of women and men. They vary among different societies and cultures, classes, ages and during different periods in history" (FAO 1997). Gender relations, in turn, are "the ways in which a culture or society defines rights, responsibilities, and the identities of men and women in relation to one another" (Bravo-Baumann, 2000). Traditionally, gender relations have placed men in positions of power, especially in spheres outside the home (e.g., business or politics), which resulted in women having fewer opportunities than men and less control over material and other resources and, ultimately, over their livelihood strategies.

---

1   Following some of the well-known writers on entrepreneurship [e.g., Richard Cantillon (1755) and Peter Drucker (1994)] we define an entrepreneur as an individual who organizes or operates a business or businesses, and entrepreneurship as the art of taking risks with an idea, one's time, or money. Agripreneur (or agripreneurship) refers to individuals (or their businesses) whose primary field is agriculture or agriculture related. Since, due to the topic of this chapter, we often refer to women agribusiness entrepreneurs, we have adopted the term "agripreneurs" as a shorthand for the term.

Given these realities, it is no surprise that research has found that, compared with their male counterparts, African female entrepreneurs face unique challenges that stem from their gender status. What are these challenges? And most importantly, how may they be overcome? Can we identify examples of successful female agripreneurs and distill from their stories some "best practices" for success? These are the questions that motivate this chapter.

The reality that women-owned SMEs facer a tougher road to success than those owned by men is even more pronounced in agribusiness than elsewhere, because agripreneurship is traditionally the domain of men. It is also more rural-based, and rural settings tend to be socially and culturally more conservative than urban areas, insisting on maintaining women's traditional domestic roles. While it is important not to overlook the challenges women entrepreneurs face, it is equally important to point out the successes. As we will see, successful women agripreneurs do exist, and we argue that it is important to recognize these successful women, particularly in the media, not only because they can be role models for others, but also because they can translate the attention into new opportunities for their own businesses.

African women entrepreneurs, like entrepreneurs around the globe, are not cut from the same cloth. They represent diverse geographic, economic, cultural, and social contexts. For example, we will see that many—though not all—of the truly successful female agripreneurs [referred to as WELAs, "Women Entrepreneurial Leaders in Agriculture," by Stearns (2013)] have somewhat rare characteristics: Most are fairly well educated, and quite a few have lived and obtained university degrees abroad before returning home to start a business. One wonders if the combination of having lived and studied outside of their society perhaps enables these women to more effectively challenge the *status quo* of gender roles and norms, putting them in a position where they may have more experience, more confidence, and greater access to networks and resources than would be the case for the majority of rural and less formally educated African women. In other words, while the achievements of WELAs should not be diminished, it would be naïve to think that their examples can be copied wholesale by others, who may not have the benefits of higher education, overseas experiences, or even a more socially liberal urban setting for a home. And yet, their examples matter: while not everything they do may be replicable, their stories have inspirational value to others, and their presence may be the seed of a growing network of women-owned agri-enterprises in Africa.

L. Chiwona-Karltun and K. Tihanyi

Our goal in this chapter is to paint a picture of women's involvement in African agribusiness, using some successful women agripreneurs as examples to illustrate our points. We begin by providing some general background on women's participation in entrepreneurship and agriculture, followed by a more detailed look at some of the key determinants of success in agripreneurship. We close by identifying a set of "best practices" that emerge from our review of successful African women agripreneurs.

Salient Features of Women's Entrepreneurship in Sub-Saharan Africa

Rates of entrepreneurship among African women

The Global Entrepreneurship Monitor (GEM) is an annual publication that provides an all-encompassing analysis of entrepreneurship worldwide. In 2012, the organization produced a special report on women entrepreneurs. The *2012 Women's Report* (Kelley et al. 2013) paints a detailed picture of female entrepreneurs, drawing data from 67 countries including 10 in Sub-Saharan Africa (Angola, Botswana, Ethiopia, Ghana, Malawi, Namibia, Nigeria, South Africa, Uganda, Zambia); thus, while not being a comprehensive report, it draws on a good cross-section of data from Africa.

African countries reported the highest total entrepreneurial activity (TEA) rates for women, a figure that includes businesses from the nascent (start-up) stage to established companies. TEA rates in Africa ranged from 6% (South Africa) to 40% (Zambia), with most over 25%. Furthermore in Africa, with rates higher than in any other region of the world, 69% of women reported that they felt that their countries had entrepreneurial opportunities and 73% said that they perceived themselves to have the abilities needed to run a business. It is important to note, however, that in Africa, more than in other regions, women start businesses out of necessity rather than opportunity. In the absence of formal employment opportunities provided by a better functioning economy, women choose self-employment because this option has relatively low barriers to entry. Just as important, the rates of established business activity (defined as being in business for at least 3.5 years) are the lowest in Africa. In short, while many African women engage in business activities and perceive themselves as capable of running a business, their businesses often do not survive long and fail at higher rates than those owned by men. Put together these observations explain why many African entrepreneurs—men and especially women—are in a seemingly endless cycle of serial start-ups. (See Box 1 for a profile of Mrs. Katundu's Bakery, a woman-owned small business in Malawi.)

Gender Differences in Economic Performance

Knowing what we do about the unequal nature of gender relations, it may not surprise us to learn that on average women entrepreneurs underperform compared with men (Bardasi et al. 2011; World Bank 2012). Why is this the case? The findings point to two sets of reasons: The first has to do with constraints outside of women's control, such as the fact that a woman finds it more difficult to obtain financing or to establish her business network. In fact, most people in Africa rely on their own savings (or funds from family members) as start-up capital, and women are least likely to have savings or any form of equity that can serve as collateral, particularly in impoverished rural areas. The second set of reasons, the findings suggest, emanates from the women themselves; that is, women tend to show preference for smaller businesses, which, in turn, receive less support as they are not seen as good investment opportunities by banks. However, the authors add that this "preference" on the part of women may in fact be a rational choice, growing

---

Box: Mrs. Chrissie Katundu's Bakery: An example of tenacity (Malawi)

Chrissie Katundu is a successful small-scale cassava agripreneur from Malawi. Her business is small, but it provides steady income for her; most importantly, it holds the potential for growth. But the road even to this level of success has not been easy. Chrissie began by opening a restaurant in 1983, followed by a second restaurant in 1986. Neither business venture survived, so Chrissie tried her hands at producing rattan chairs. Unfortunately, this business also failed. Undeterred, she returned to her roots in the restaurant business and opened a bakery in 1999. One of the main challenges for the bakery was the high price of wheat flour at the time, which was limiting her operations. A turning point came when she learned about substituting cassava for wheat flour. She experimented with cassava flour and made scones from the sweet cassava–wheat flour mix. Chrissie's bakery business has been in operation for over 15 years and, while it is still small, she has obtained equipment from a nongovernmental organization, technical support from a university, and business training through various short courses. Chrissie's example illustrates two key features of agripreneurship in Africa—one, the fact that many entrepreneurs are serial entrepreneurs, trying one business after another, and, two, that tenacity and hard work can take them quite far.

Source: Chiwona-Karltun and Brimer 2015

out of women's recognition that they can devote only limited energies to their business when they are expected to shoulder the majority of child care and household work as well.

Importantly, "after we control for other key enterprise characteristics—ensuring that we compare like with like—it is encouraging to find no or few significant differences in performance of female and male entrepreneurs" (Hallward-Driemeier 2013, 38). (A clear illustration of this is the case of Hillside Green Growers and Exporters Ltd., profiled in Box 2.) Indeed, productivity differences between female-owned and male-owned businesses are often explained by differences in access to productive resources, and these differences are primarily a function of the business size and sector of operation rather than a gender-specific factor (World Bank 2012). The issue of formal vs. informal enterprises also confounds this question. Among African firms in urban areas, the median female-owned firm in the formal sector has one-fifth the start-up capital of the median male-owned firm, but it has five times more start-up capital than the median female-owned firm in the informal sector (Chirwa 2008).

Determinants of Success for Women-Owned Agribusinesses in Africa

While the 2012 GEM report (Kelley et al. 2013) and other sources on women's participation in entrepreneurship are useful, they lack an explicit focus on agribusinesses. Similarly, when development organizations look at women's participation in the agricultural spheres, their focus is almost exclusively on agriculture, paying little attention to agribusiness. The result is a paucity of research on women in agribusiness to date that leaves us with a relatively small number of sources to draw on to identify the factors that determine if a woman-owned agribusiness becomes a success. Thankfully, we can supplement these findings with our own experiences of working with women agripreneurs through the Making Markets Matter training program. While these observations do not represent formal research, our anecdotal evidence in most cases confirms the research findings.

Access to Land

Women perform 70% to 80% of the agricultural work in Africa (Stearns 2013), yet the rate of land ownership by women is significantly less due to

Box: Eunice Mwongera of Hillside Green Growers and Exporters Ltd. (Kenya)

Eunice K. Mwongera is the owner and director of Hillside Green Growers and Exporters Ltd., a fruit and vegetable company. Established in 1998, the company, although still classified an SME, has seen impressive growth over the years. As Mwongera recalls, it all started when she was on her way to Dubai to purchase computer hardware for import into Kenya. On that flight she sat next to a man who told her of opportunities in the horticultural industry for entrepreneurs in the Middle East. "I was intrigued. My entrepreneurial curiosity kicked in, and I told myself that instead of bringing goods into Kenya, why not start exporting what Kenya has to offer?" Upon landing in Dubai, Mwongera headed to the fruit and vegetable markets, and by the time she left, she had secured her first order of mangoes. She recalls: "My first buyer took a big chance with me. I convinced him I could ship him mangoes, and I knew I had to deliver on that promise. We sourced the product and sent him the shipment in just a few short weeks. From that, Hillside was born."

From such beginnings grew Hillside, which now has 25 permanent employees and provides income to 150 part-time workers. The initial order of mangoes grew into a broad product line of fresh vegetables, including French green beans, snow peas, sugar snaps, chili peppers, eggplant, and okra, as well as fruits such as mangoes, avocados, passion fruit, and pineapple. Hillside's main export markets are in the Middle East (Dubai, Kuwait, Qatar,) and Europe (Norway, the Netherlands, and the United Kingdom), as well the local Kenyan market. In 12 years, the company's annual turnover grew to more than US$500,000. Hillside is also GlobalGap certified.

When talking to Mwongera, one thing that shines through is her commitment to people at all levels of the business. As she puts it, "The growth of the employees is the growth of the company." Many of the part-time workers come from low-income communities around Nairobi. Hillside partners with rural smallholder farmers to grow vegetables and fruits, and at present the company works with 500 to 800 farmer groups and individual agents. Hillside also supports farmers' access to inputs, including certified seeds, and access to finance through a partnership with Equity Bank. The company facilitates training, seminars, and workshops on good agricultural practices and GlobalGAP certification.

Source: Based on a case study by Mabaya and Cramer (2014)

various cultural and historical reasons. Most women work land that belongs to their husbands, sons, or the community. Of course, land ownership is not a necessary prerequisite of agripreneurship; agripreneurs that work with contract farmers do not necessarily need land, nor do urban-based businesses that produce value-added products. Even in such cases, however, land may confer a certain level of independence and may be used as collateral when applying for business loans, opening up opportunities for funding beyond microloans. Further, land ownership has been shown to give women access to various producers or resource management associations (Ashby et al. 2008).

If women own land, their status in the home is enhanced, giving them greater bargaining power (Agarwal 1997). Women who own land are also likely to contribute more toward food in the family than men, which could positively influence household nutritional outcomes and have ripple effects in broader society (Doss 2006). All this is likely to provide positive examples for younger generations, in the process promoting—and cementing—change in social norms.

Access to Inputs, New Technologies, Education, and Training

While land may be the first requisite of a successful agribusiness (whether as a resource or as collateral), inputs and new technologies may be a close second. Probably no one needs convincing that in recent years the most revolutionary technology in Africa has been the mobile telephone, enabling access to relevant information and services, such as banking, to make informed decisions (Jack and Suri 2011). Despite such advances, on average, women agripreneurs have significantly less access to inputs and information than men. In fact, a study found that at present globally there are 300 million fewer women than men with access to mobile technology (Mehta et al. 2011). Studies (Huyer 2005; Slater and Tacchi 2005; Garrido and Roman 2006; Maier and Nair-Reichert 2007) show that women who own mobile technology feel more confident and more willing to take chances, and since entrepreneurship is about taking risks, giving women greater access to and literacy with mobile technology seems like an obvious area for increased focus and investment. For example, in Kenya the Women Enterprise Fund has joined forces with M-Pesa, so that women can make their loan repayments directly from their mobile phones (Mwangi, 2012).

At the same time, we see that the real successful businesses—such as those profiled in this chapter—have overcome the issue of access to inputs, underlining the finding of development organizations like FAO and the World Bank that, given the same inputs, women are at least as productive as men (FAO 2011; World Bank 2012). This statement about productivity is also significant because organizations like FAO estimate that if women had equal access to inputs and information, their contributions would significantly increase their countries' overall economic productivity.

When women are excluded from owning—or using—new technologies it is often due to cost (Ashby et al. 2008). It is also the case that women tend to be more risk-averse than men when it comes to adopting new technologies (Ashby et al. 2008; Kelley et al. 2013). But again, while this is probably true for many women-owned small businesses—most of which tend to be on less-than-secure financial footing—the WELAs have found a way to access—and harness—the latest technologies and may be just as much risk-takers as their male counterparts.

A related issue is that of education. While higher education is not a prerequisite of entrepreneurship, we have noted that many successful female agripreneurs are well educated, often possessing university degrees. This separates them from the "average" African woman, who is less educated than her male counterpart (Kinkingninhoun-Mêdagbé et al. 2008; Barham and Chitemi 2009). Our story here is somewhat encouraging since in many countries the education gap between men and women is closing, and closing fast. A particularly promising development for agripreneurship is the growing number of women in agriculture in tertiary institutions, as both students and staff. Still, there is a way to go, as the education gap persists in some countries, particularly in rural areas (FAO 2011).

Access to Finance
Studies consistently report that African women, in particular those in rural areas, receive smaller amounts of financing (Ashby et al. 2008) and have lower returns on investment than men [though the lower returns are generally due to the specific business area chosen by women, which by its nature generates lower returns (Kelley et al. 2013)]. Also, women are primarily microfinance clients rather than recipients of larger loans (Ashby et al. 2008), in large part due to a lack of land ownership.

Access to inputs and finance are closely correlated. If a woman has access to better inputs, the quality of her products is likely to improve, which, presumably, leads to increased income and profits, opening the door to securing larger loans on more favorable terms. This is the opportunity that many successful female large agripreneurs have been able to take advantage of. They have managed to secure large enough loans—or other means of financing—to open the door to significant growth. Interestingly, in her study on WELAs, Stearns (2013) reports somewhat conflicting findings. On the one hand, the women she interviewed indicated that, when they did

L. Chiwona-Karltun and K. Tihanyi

receive financing, they felt they had done so on the merit of their business proposition. Yet, when they talked about unsuccessful bids, some did cite the fact that they were women as a possible reason for being turned down. It is impossible to know the truth based on the information available, but it may be that gender discrimination at this level is not always obvious. Whatever the case, the women Stearns interviewed indicated that they preferred not to dwell on the question of whether being a woman disadvantages them or not—they simply keep moving forward. We have heard similar sentiments from successful women agripreneurs in our Making Markets Matter program.

Access to Markets

Market access is consistently recognized as one of the key challenges facing agribusinesses in developing countries. Poor infrastructure, high cost of transportation, and lack of market intelligence are among the key challenges cited, especially in the case of agriculture and agribusiness, where the entrepreneur may be located far from major urban centers.

While market access is a challenge for men *and* women, research shows that accessing markets, especially new markets, is consistently more difficult for female business owners. In the case of a microbusiness, in which the owner is also responsible for marketing activities, women are often at a disadvantage as they simply have less time to devote to marketing; competing obligations of child care and household responsibilities leave little time for running one's business. Put simply, assuming that men and women spend equal amounts of time on production, men will have time left over to explore marketing opportunities, whereas the rest of a woman's day is generally taken up by household chores (Dolan 2001).

Larger, more established women-owned companies are likely to have a dedicated marketing manager, who may or may not be a woman. But even in this case, the women owners are likely to be heavily involved with promoting the enterprise and its products. In fact, a notable shared characteristic of WELAs identified by Stearns (2013) is the availability of a supportive home (which includes household help and may very well include a supportive spouse or partner, too) to enable women to devote their attention to running their business.

Another important aspect of marketing that pertains specifically to women agripreneurs is the experience of having to enter—and succeed—in a world that traditionally has been—and largely still is—a man's world. Some female agripreneurs in the Making Markets Matter program have spoken about having to overcome a feeling of intimidation as they encountered men in business dealings who did not take them seriously—at least initially—precisely because they were women. Unfortunately, studies have also documented cases of sexual harassment against women in exchange for favorable entrepreneurial outcomes (Mordi et al. 2010), a barrier that has not received enough attention. Whether more or less serious, the fact is that business activities like marketing bring women into contact with social norms and forces that tend to favor men over women. The concept of social capital is useful to discuss here.

Access to Social Capital and Trust

While access to land, finance, inputs, and markets is quantifiable and therefore easier to grasp, there are some additional factors that, while they may be more difficult to define and, more importantly, to measure, are in fact crucial to understanding why gender equality in agribusiness (and agriculture in general) is elusive. Understanding these concepts may hold the key to unlocking the potential of women-owned businesses.

One such concept is social capital. Putnam (2006) defined the term as "social networks and the associated norms of reciprocity and trustworthiness." Another definition is "investment in social relations with expected returns in the marketplace" (Lin 2001). Using either of the definitions, it is clear that social capital is critical to entrepreneurship. Further, social capital is developed over time, through series of interactions among individuals in a community. To the extent that women do not have the same amount of time as men to devote to building business relationships, it would appear that they stand to be marginalized in the process of building the social capital necessary for a successful business. Further, as mentioned above, even if women had the time, they may encounter resistance from men if they tried to enter traditionally male-dominated spaces.

While largely correct, this view signals that social capital is of one type—that cultivated by men for men, and which is not readily open to women. (See the story of Jacky Goliath of South Africa in Box 3 for an illustration .) But there is another way to view social capital, one revealed by the Ethiopian coffee producer Mistlal in her interview with Stearns (2013). When asked whether she considered being a woman a disadvantage in running a business, Mistlal said that, in fact, she viewed being a woman as a plus. Because she works mostly with female contract farmers, she feels that she, as a woman, can better relate to her contractors than a man could. This illustrates that one way for women agripreneurs to succeed in a traditionally male-dominated world is to capitalize on women's strengths as communicators and listeners, instead of trying to conform to ideas of traditional, masculine ways of running a business.

While social capital deals more with the collective value of social networks, the aspect of trust[2] is one of the most fundamental factors for women's participation in agripreneurship. A study from Tanzania revealed that female entrepreneurs ranked trust and loyalty above making a larger profit (Mehta et al. 2011). In other words, women prized the trust developed over time in building their business networks, believing that trust would lead to long-lasting and strong business bonds.

Box 3: Jacky Goliath of DeFynne (South Africa)

In 2001, a young horticulturalist named Jacqueline "Jacky" Goliath participated in the inaugural Making Markets Matter program. Fast-forward 13 years and Goliath is the co-owner and managing director of DeFynne Nursery, a wholesale nursery located in South Africa's Western Cape that produces indigenous potted plants, fruit trees, and other ornamentals for the local horticultural and agricultural industry.

By Goliath's own admission, when she started in 2001 with 1,000 plants in a small backyard nursery, she never dreamed that it would grow into a 600,000 plant production nursery that employs 25 employees and exhibits at trade shows in Japan, the United States, and South Africa. Nor did she see that, in 2012, the nursery would relocate to a large farm and expand its operations to include plums and other fruits destined for export.

What Goliath did see was a need in the marketplace that matched her training and passion. Thirteen years and much hard work later, this MMM alumna is the proud owner of a vibrant company with an exciting future. When Goliath recently shared her experiences with the latest group of MMM participants, she recalled how initially she was quite intimidated, when, in business negotiations, some men clearly did not take her seriously because she was a woman. Goliath joked that her short stature did not help; but she stood up taller and decided not to let the unfamiliar environment—and the men—intimidate her. The story of DeFynne clearly shows that this woman, who had both the requisite education and experience working with plants, had what it took to build a successful enterprise.

---

2   The issue of trust also features in the chapter on Strategic Planning in this volume. There the importance of trust between employer and employee is highlighted.

The challenge of issues such as social capital and trust is that they tend to be more elusive—and therefore more difficult to influence—than issues such as access to land or inputs. A recent World Bank report aptly names them "sticky areas," noting that change in these areas would require changing "deeply entrenched gender roles and social norms about who is responsible for care and housework in the home, and what is 'acceptable' for women and men to study, do, and aspire to. And these gaps tend to be reproduced across generations" (World Bank 2012, 13).

Conclusion and Best Practices

This chapter has shown that gender relations often affect women's and men's rights, roles, and responsibilities differently, and that they translate into different kinds of opportunities and constraints in running a successful business. But we have seen evidence that, given an equal playing field, women are just as capable as men of being successful entrepreneurs. Unfortunately the playing field is not yet even, but slowly the number of successful African women agripreneurs is growing. Using the word "pioneer" is not an overstatement when talking about these women; they are, indeed, entering new territory and forging a new path, which it is hoped others will be able to follow. In some sense, these women are learning to play a "men's game," while in other ways they are building on their existing strengths to move their business forward. While each case is different with different components of success, the following Best Practices emerge.

- **Education matters!** Although not all successful women agripreneurs are highly educated, the majority are. Having an education comes not only with knowledge, but also with increased confidence, a sense of independence and accomplishment, all of which are useful qualities for successful entrepreneurs.
- **Successful women agripreneurs are risk-takers**. By risk-taking we do not mean a reckless pursuit of business opportunities without careful thought, but running a successful business takes a certain amount of risk, and successful women agripreneurs are not afraid to take some risks.
- **Successful women agripreneurs recruit—and receive—support** from spouse, extended family, and, importantly, from other women. They recognize that they cannot do it alone and are in the fortunate position of having support available to them in the form of family

members and/or paid help. In short, they are not afraid to ask for help.

- **Successful women agripreneurs rely on and play up their strengths:** listening to others, connecting with others, and recognizing the needs of others. They do not feel pressured to be or act like "typical" men, but rather feel comfortable in their skin as women.
- **Successful women agripreneurs want to be judged on their merit.** They do not let themselves dwell on how being a woman may disadvantage them; they keep pushing forward.
- **Successful women agripreneurs are optimists.** Being an entrepreneur, even in the best of circumstances, means facing—and overcoming—a series of challenges, and optimism is essential for staying in the game.

Sources

Agarwal, B. (1997). "Bargaining" and Gender Relations: Within and beyond the Household. *Feminist Economics* 3(1): 1–51.

Akudugu, M., I. Egyir, and A. Mensah-Bonsu (2009). Women Farmers' Access to Credit from Rural Banks in Ghana. *Agricultural Finance Review* 69(3): 284–299.

Ashby, J., M. Hartl, Y. Lambrou, G. Larson, A. Lubbock, E. Pehu, and C. Ragasa (2008). Investing in Women as Drivers of Agricultural Growth. *Agriculture and Rural Development.* IFAD/The World Bank.

Bardasi, E., S. Sabarwal, and K. Terrell (2011). How Do Female Entrepreneurs Perform? Evidence from Three Developing Regions. *Small Bus Econ* 37: 417–441.

Barham, J. and C. Chitemi (2009). Collective Action Initiatives to Improve Marketing Performance: Lessons from Farmer Groups in Tanzania. *Food Policy* 34: 53–59.

Bravo-Baumann, H. (2000). *Capitalisation of experiences on the contribution of livestock projects to gender issues. Working Document.* Bern, Switzerland: Swiss Agency for Development and Cooperation.

Cantillon, Richard (1755). *Essai sur la nature du commerce en général.* London: MacMillan.

Carpano, F. (2011). *Strengthening Women's Access to Land into IFAD projects: The Rwanda Experience.* Nyarutarama, Rwanda: Rwanda Initiative for Sustainable Development.

Chiwona-Karltun & Brimer, 2015. Cassava entrepreneurship in rural Malawi. African Journal of Food, Agriculture, Nutrition and Development (forthcoming).

Chirwa, E. W. (2008). Effects of Gender on the Performance of Micro and Small Enterprises in Malawi. *Development Southern Africa* 25(3): 347–362.

Commonwealth Secretariat (June 2001). Gender Mainstreaming in Agriculture and Rural Development: A Reference Manual for Governments and Other Stakeholders. Gender Management System Series.

Development Alternatives Inc. (1999). Sowing the Seeds of Opportunity: Women in Agribusiness. *GenderReach Information Bulletin* 7.

Dolan, C. (2001). The 'Good Wife': Struggles over Resources in the Kenyan Horticultural Sector. *The Journal of Development Studies* 37(3): 39.

Doss, C. (2006). The Effects of Intrahousehold Property Ownership on Expenditure Patterns in Ghana. *Journal of African Economies* 15(1): 149–180.

Drucker, Peter F. (1994). *Innovation and Entrepreneurship: Practice and Principles*. Oxford: Butterworth-Heinemann.

FAO (1997). Gender: the key to sustainability and food security. SD Dimensions, May 1997 (available at www.fao.org/sd).

FAO (2011). *The State of Food and Agriculture; Women in Agriculture 2011*.Rome, Italy: FAO.

Garrido, M., and R. Roman (2006). Women in Latin America: Appropriating ICTs for Social Change. *In*: Hafkin, N., and S. Huyer (eds.), *Cinderella or Cyberella? Empowering Women in the Knowledge Society* (165–190). Bloomfield, CT: Kumarian Press.

Hallward-Driemeier, M. (2013). *Enterprising Women. Expanding Economic Opportunities in Africa*. Washington, DC: The World Bank.

Horan, D. (2013a). *How Stronger Land Use Rights Can Curb Global Hunger*. Devex.org, Aug. 29, 2013.

Horan, D. (2013b). *Why Women Should Own Their Land*. Devex.org, Sept. 6, 2013.

Huyer, S. (2005). Women, ICT and the Information Society: Global Perspectives and Initiatives. Proceedings of the International Symposium on Women and ICT: Creating Global Transformation. June 12–14. New York: Association for Computing Machinery (ACM). doi>10.1145/1117417.1117418.

Jack, W., and T. Suri (2011). *Mobile Money: The Economics of M-PESA* (No. w16721). National Bureau of Economic Research.

Kelley, D., C. Brush, P. Greene, and Y. Litovsky (2013). *Global Entrepreneurship Monitor (GEM) 2012 Women's Report*. London: Global Entrepreneurship Research Association (GERA).

Kinkingninhoun-Mêdagbé, F., A. Diagne, F. Simtowe, A. Agboh-Noameshie, and P. Adégbola (2008). Gender Discrimination and Its Impact on Income, Productivity, and Technical Efficiency: Evidence from Benin. *Agric Hum Values* 27: 57–69.

Lin, Nan (2001). *Social Capital*. Cambridge, UK: Cambridge University Press.

Mabaya, E., and L. Cramer. (2014) Growth in a Globalized Industry: The Case of Hillside Green Growers & Exporters Ltd. *International Food and Agribusiness Management Review (IFAMR), Special Issue: African Agribusiness on the Move* 17 Special Issue B: 201-206.

Maier, S., and U. Nair-Reichert (2007). Empowering Women through ICT-based Business Initiatives: An Overview of Best Practices in E-commerce/E-Retailing projects. *Information Technologies and International Development* 4(2): 43–60.

Mehta, Khanjan, L. Semali, and A. Maretzki (2011). The primacy of trust in the social networks and livelihoods of women agro-entrepreneurs in northern Tanzania. *African Journal of Food, Agriculture, Nutrition and Development* 11 (6): 5361-5372 .

Meinzen-Dick, R., J. Behrman, P. Menon, and A. Quisumbing (2011). Gender: A Key Dimension Linking Agricultural Programs to Improved Nutrition and Health. Leveraging Agriculture for Improving Nutrition and Health 2020 Conference Brief 9 (Feb).

Minniti, M. (2010). Female Entrepreneurship and Economic Activity. *European Journal of Development Research* 22: 294–312.

Mordi, C., R. Simpson, S. Singh, and C. Okafor (2010). A Barrier That Has Not Received Enough Attention. The Role of Cultural Values in Understanding the Challenges Faced by Female Entrepreneurs in Nigeria. *Gender in Management: An International Journal* 25(1): 5–21.

Mwangi, P.G. (2012) Loan Repayment Made Easier For Kenyan Women Entrepreneurs. *Think M-Pesa*. http://www.thinkm-pesa.com/2012/02/loan-repayment-made-easier-for-kenyan.html (accessed on March 26, 2015)

Putnam, R. (2007). E Pluribus Unum: Diversity and Community in the Twenty-first Century. The 2006 Johan Skytte Prize Lecture. *Scandinavian Political Studies* 30(2): 137–174.

Slater, D., and J. Tacchi (2005). *ICT Innovations for Poverty Reduction*. New Delhi: United Nations Educational, Scientific and Cultural Organization, Asia Pacific Regional Bureau for Communication and Information.

Stearns, M. (2013). How Women Are Succeeding as Entrepreneurial Leaders in Agriculture: Ten Case Studies from Sub-Saharan Africa and Latin America. Working Paper prepared for the Global Gender Program, The George Washington University for Presentation at the GW Global Entrepreneurship Research and Policy Conference in Washington, DC, October 17–19.

Swedish International Agricultural Network Initiative (SIANI) (2012). *Transforming Gender Relations in Agriculture in Sub-Saharan Africa: Promising Approaches.* Sweden: SIANI.

The World Bank (2012). *World Development Report 2012.* Washington, DC: World Bank.

The World Bank (2013). *Growing Africa Unlocking the Potential of Agribusiness.* Washington, DC: World Bank.

CONTRIBUTORS

Maureen Bandama holds a BS degree in Agriculture and Natural Resources with a major in Agribusiness from Africa University, Zimbabwe and an MS degree in Agricultural Economics from Stellenbosch University. Before joining Stellenbosch University, she spent two years as a compliance monitor (Agricultural and Financial Services sector) at the Reserve Bank of Zimbabwe. Maureen joined Market Matters Inc. in January 2011 as Regional Agribusiness Program Coordinator–Southern Africa. In this capacity, her responsibilities include developing and coordinating MM Inc.'s capacity building program in Africa and various research and administrative activities. Among other things, she is currently involved in a survey of emerging farms and agribusinesses in South Africa, carried out jointly by the National Agricultural Marketing Council and Market Matters Inc.

Linley Chiwona-Karltun holds a BS in Food Nutrition and Institutional Management, an MS in Nutrition, and a PhD in International Health. She is a lecturer and research fellow at The Swedish University of Agricultural Sciences (SLU) in Sweden. In 2002 she cofounded the Chinangwa ndi Mbatata Roots and Tubers Enterprise (CMRTE) in Malawi, which has a membership of over 3000 farmers, more than 80% of whom are women. CMRTE empowers its members with skills and information to manage, produce, and process cassava, to develop nutritious products, and to commercialize their products. CMRTE has received several awards in recognition of its commitment to cassava agroprocessing and entrepreneurial achievements.

She is also a founding member of the Network of African-European Women Scientists (NAWES), The Association of African Agricultural Professionals in the Diaspora–Europe (AAAPD-E) and serves on several editorial and international boards.

Ralph D. Christy is the founder of Market Matters, Inc. and is Director of the Cornell International Institute for Food, Agriculture and Development and Professor of Emerging Markets at Cornell University in Ithaca, New York, where he teaches and conducts food marketing research and educational programs on the economic performance of markets and distribution systems. He has advised industry leaders and public policymakers on food marketing strategies, economic development, and the organization of the global food economy. A PhD graduate of Michigan State University's Department of Agricultural Economics, he is a past president of the American Agricultural Economics Association, and past board member of the Winthrop Rockefeller Foundation, WinRock International, and the Agribusiness Capital Fund. He is the author of *A Century of Service: Land Grant Colleges and Universities, 1890–1990* (1992); and *Achieving Sustainable Communities in a Global Economy* (2004).

Njeri Gakonyo is an Agricultural Economist with a wide range of interests and engagements including Africa's economic and social progress, agriculture, environment, youth, strategy, faith, and leadership. Currently she is a consultant to the Resource Mobilisation unit at the Alliance for a Green Revolution in Africa (AGRA). Prior to working at AGRA, she facilitated strategy development for both business and nonprofit organizations on a consultancy basis in Kenya, Tanzania, Mozambique, and Malawi. She previously worked as associate director at Lattice Consulting Limited, a corporate finance and strategy firm in Nairobi. She studied economics at the undergraduate level at Grinnell College and agricultural economics at Cornell University at Master's and PhD levels. She is the immediate past board chair of the Green Belt Movement (GBM) and serves on the board of the Wangari Maathai Institute for Peace and Environmental Studies (WMI) at the University of Nairobi.

Jose Jackson has a master's and PhD in Food Science from Cornell University and Michigan State University in the USA. Her research interests are in the processing and quality evaluation of fruits and vegetable products. She has more than 10 years' experience in academia, industry, and government. Currently she is a scientist in the Food Group of the Centre for Scientific Research, Indigenous Knowledge and Innovation (CesrIKi) at the University of Botswana (UB). In addition to her scientific experience, she also has extensive experience in research management in her role as the deputy director of research at UB. She has served as director of research at a food research institute in Botswana and lecturer of Food Science at the University of the West Indies in Jamaica. She is the Botswana representative at International Union of Food Science and Technology and is a member of Institute of Food Technologists, where she chaired the Fruit and Vegetable Products Division.

Mohammad Karaan is a graduate of Stellenbosch University, where he obtained a BS in Agriculture in 1987, an MS in 1993, and a PhD in 2003. He joined the Development Bank of Southern Africa in Johannesburg as an economist and later returned to Stellenbosch to join the Rural Foundation as Head of Research. In 1997 he joined the University of Stellenbosch as a lecturer in the Agricultural Faculty, where he has served as Dean of the Faculty of AgriSciences and Vice-Rector. He has also served as an advisor to the public sector in the following capacities: chair of the National Agricultural Marketing Council (2005–2007), vice-chair of the National Agricultural Marketing Council (2007–2009), chair of the Ministerial Committee on Agricultural Marketing (2007), consultant to various local authorities, coordinator of an executive training program for African agribusinesses, and president of the Agricultural Economics Association of South Africa (2008–2009). In the private sector his involvement includes directorships with KaapAgri, Bester Feed & Grain Exchange, Agricol Seeds, Southern Oils Ltd, Roman Bay Aquafarm, Pioneer Foods, and the Melsetter Group.

Ndunge Kiiti is a Professor of International Development at Houghton College, in Houghton, NY and Adjunct Faculty at Emory University's Rollins School of Public Health, Department of Global Health, in Atlanta, GA. With a key focus on Africa and Latin America, Dr. Kiiti's work involves research, teaching, and publishing in the areas of communication, education, health and development. Currently, her collaborative research projects highlight the use of mobile money technology by women's microcredit groups and the 'Jua Kali' or informal business sector in Kenya. She serves on the boards of MAP International, a global health organization, and Jericho Road Community Health Center, both based in the U.S. Dr. Kiiti has a PhD in Communication from Cornell University, Ithaca, NY which included a one year study in International Health at the John's Hopkins School of Public Health, Baltimore, MD.

Edward Mabaya is an academic and a development practitioner. He is involved in several programs that seek to improve the lives of African farmers through private enterprises. He established and coordinates the Seeds of Development Program, a business development services and networking program for emerging seed companies in East and Southern Africa. As a research associate in the Department of Applied Economics and Management at Cornell University, he conducts research on food marketing and distribution, seed systems, and the role of efficient agricultural markets in Africa's economic development. He is assistant director at the Cornell International Institute for Food, Agriculture, and Development. He earned his MS and PhD degrees in Agricultural Economics at Cornell University and his BS from the University of Zimbabwe. In 2007, he was an Archbishop Desmond Tutu Leadership Fellow at the African Leadership Institute at Oxford University. During 2010–2011, he was a visiting researcher at Stellenbosch University in South Africa.

Onkutlwile Othata is a lecturer in the Department of Accounting and Finance at the University of Botswana. He has been with the university since 1993 and has lectured in both managerial and financial accounting. His research interests are in the areas of accounting and accountability in both organizational and social contexts. His research has been disseminated both locally and internationally in conferences, workshops, and scholarly publications. In addition, he has provided consultancy and advisory services in various business environments.

Quinetta M. Roberson is a Professor of Management in the Villanova School of Business at Villanova University, prior to which, she was an Associate Professor of Human Resource Studies at Cornell University. She has a PhD in Organizational Behavior as well as MBA and BS degrees in Finance. She also has practical work experience, both as a financial analyst and a consultant. Her research, which is on fairness in work teams and strategic diversity management, has appeared in the top scholarly journals in Management and Applied Psychology. She is also the editor of the Handbook of Diversity in the Workplace (2013) published by Oxford Press and delivered a TED talk on "The Science of Inclusion". She teaches courses globally on leadership, talent management and diversity at the undergraduate, graduate and executive levels.

Krisztina Tihanyi divides her time between the 'real world' and academia. At Market Matters Inc. she is chief operating officer. In this capacity, she coordinates the organization's agribusiness training portfolio and publication activities. She is also in charge of grant writing and administration, as well as fundraising and financial management. At Cornell University she holds visiting appointments at the Institute for African Development and the Cornell International Institute for Food, Agriculture, and Development. Her background includes degrees in Psychology, International Peace Studies, and Anthropology. A PhD graduate of Cornell University, she has a keen interest in developing educational programs that lead to social and economic transformation. She has written the book *Blending in the Rainbow Nation* (2006) (an account of post-Apartheid reconciliation and racial integration in South Africa) and co-edited the volume *Case Studies of Emerging Farmers and Agribusinesses in South Africa* (2011).

Norbert Wilson is Professor of Agricultural Economics at Auburn University, where he has been on faculty since 1999. He received a BS in Agricultural Economics from the University of Georgia. He went on to earn an MS in Agricultural Economics from the University of London, Wye College. He attended the University of California, Davis, where he completed his doctorate in Agricultural and Resource Economics. He has worked at the Organization for Economic Cooperation and Development (OECD) in Paris, France, where he analyzed international trade and food safety and structural adjustment. As a faculty member at Auburn, he teaches courses in the area of agribusiness: international trade, price analysis and sustainability. His research portfolio includes agricultural trade and hunger domestically and abroad.

www.ingramcontent.com/pod-product-compliance
Lightning Source LLC
Chambersburg PA
CBHW032002190326
41520CB00007B/333